Liz Cowell has over 30 years' experience in the practice of Family Law. For the past 6 years she has lectured on the subject of spousal maintenance in the jurisdiction of England and Wales to fellow Family Practitioners. She has had experience of sitting on the Child Support Act Tribunal and has sat as a Deputy District Judge since 2000. Her interest in the Family Court's approach to spousal maintenance was sparked following anecdotal research done during the noughties which demonstrated that there was a wide difference in the approach to spousal maintenance across the jurisdiction followed by a Resolution conference on the topic which further highlighted the problems that many practitioners were encountering. At the same time, she had built up a practice assisting clients with problems with the Child Support Agency (as it was then) and subsequently, she assists parents with respect to issues concerning the Child Maintenance Service.

A Practical Guide to Spousal Maintenance

A Practical Guide to Spousal Maintenance

Elizabeth Cowell LLB
Deputy District Judge
Family Law Arbitrator
Fellow of the International Academy of Family Lawyers
Solicitor McAlister Family Law

Law Brief Publishing

Published 2019 by Law Brief Publishing, an imprint of Law Brief Publishing Ltd
30 The Parks
Minehead
Somerset
TA24 8BT

www.lawbriefpublishing.com

Paperback: 978-1-912687-15-2

PREFACE

There was a recent report in The Times about the wife of the shoe magnate Ferruccio Ferragarno trying to get her divorce proceedings determined in this jurisdiction. Such reports perpetuate the myth that our courts are ridiculously generous and that London is the "Divorce Capital" of the world.

In fact for the great majority of divorcees the discretion given to our judiciary has allowed for the law to follow, albeit slowly the enormous changes in society since 1973.I hope that my book provides an explanation as to why every case is different and ultimately why a discretionary approach to financial support is far better than a rigid formulaic approach.

Around 2010 there was a lot of concern amongst family practitioners that the judges in the Principle Registry were being far more generous towards wives than the judges in the county courts outside of the capital. The advent of The Family Court which prevents the wily practitioner from issuing proceedings for wives in London has ironed that out and is reflected in the recent case law. Indeed it looks as if Senora Ferragarno will have to let the Italian Courts deal with her case.

Although fundamentally I am in favour of a discretionary system I am aware that it can make it harder to give advice to clients, after all they are paying a lot of money to be told that its not possible to give an exact figure for maintenance. I hope that my book will help my fellow practitioners to provide that advise with confidence.

The law stated in this book is believed to be up-to-date at 2nd April 2019.

I would like to dedicate my book to my wonderfully supportive husband Lawrence Yusupoff. Living with a clinical psychologist is enormously helpful as I know that I can go home to someone who understands the emotional turmoil that the family practitioner navigates with his or her clients every day. Lawrence has been my rock throughout my career and very patient whilst this book has been written. I would also like to thank my colleagues at McAlister Family Law they too have supported me on this journey, in particular my amazing colleague Carol McGuire without whose help I could not have completed this project.

Liz Cowell
April 2019

CONTENTS

Chapter One	Introduction	1
Chapter Two	History	5
Chapter Three	The Matrimonial Causes Act 1973 ("MCA 1973")	13
Chapter Four	The Statute and the Rules	17
Chapter Five	Maintenance Pending Suit and Interim Periodical Payments	23
Chapter Six	Applications Pursuant to Section 23 Matrimonial Causes Act 1973 for Periodical Payments of Maintenance	35
Chapter Seven	The Clean Break Problem	41
Chapter Eight	The Problems Surrounding Sharing the Payers Income	53
Chapter Nine	Needs Are Elastic	61
Chapter Ten	Bonuses and How They Affect Maintenance	71
Chapter Eleven	Cohabitation	77
Chapter Twelve	Variation of Periodical Payments	83
Chapter Thirteen	Capitalisation	87
Chapter Fourteen	The Treatment of Bonuses in Financial Settlement	93

Chapter Fifteen   Pensions   99

Chapter Sixteen   Bankruptcy   103

Chapter Seventeen   The Child Support Act 1991   105

CHAPTER ONE
INTRODUCTION

For those practicing family law in the jurisdiction of England and Wales ("this jurisdiction") it is a given that the issue as to whether one spouse or civil partner should pay the other maintenance after the breakdown of a marriage or civil partnership should be considered by the court.

This is not so in many other jurisdictions. Indeed, across the border in Scotland whilst there is some ability to provide maintenance to an ex-spouse it is only for a limited period of time and to meet needs only. Furthermore, only the matrimonial acquest is divided equally and there is no ability to use other assets as a resource to support an ex-spouse in the same way as there is in this jurisdiction. So, for example if a Scottish footballer with a very high income who had substantial assets acquired before his marriage were to proceed to a divorce, his ex-wife could not expect to be maintained indefinitely following a marriage breakdown. Her capital settlement would be limited to an equal division of the matrimonial acquest.

In this jurisdiction we need to be mindful of the popular wave of belief that Scotland has got it right and that it is time for a change in our legislation.

One argument in favour of a change is that the legislation has not been amended since the amendments made to the Matrimonial Causes Act 1973 ("The MCA 1973") by the Matrimonial and Family Proceedings Act 1984 ("The 1984 Act"). So strong is the belief, in some quarters, that our discretionary system needs to be overhauled if not abandoned altogether that a private members bill pursued by Baroness Deech may mean the (Financial Provision) Bill [HL] 2016/2017/UK first introduced in February 2014 and which passed its second reading on the

27th January 2019 will eventually become the law. The bill now awaits a line by line examination at committee stage.

Baroness Deech's bill aims to make financial provision;

"simpler, more certain and democratic".

With respect to the issue of spousal maintenance the aim of the bill is to restrict any provision to a total of 5 years save in exceptional circumstances.

As well as there being strongly held beliefs about the need for reform as to how and when a spouse is entitled to maintenance there is another issue that needs to be taken into account by those practicing family law.

That issue is the inescapable fact that society has changed a great deal since 1984. The beauty of a system that is discretionary is that it can adapt to such changes through case law which reflects the same indeed as stated by Lord Nichols in Miller -v- Miller; McFarlane -v- McFarland [2006] UK [HL] 24 [2006] 2WLR1283 1FLR 186 at paragraph 4.

"Fairness is an allusive concept it is an instinctive response to a given set of facts. Ultimately it is grounded in social and moral values. These values or attitudes can be stated. They cannot be justified or refuted by any objective process of logic or reasoning. Moreover, they change from one generation to the next it is not surprising therefore that in the present context there can be different views on requirements of fairness in any particular case".

His point being that the breadth of the discretion given to the court by Section 25 MCA 1973 as amended and Section 25 A enables the court to deal with financial provision as fairly as possible for each unique family in its particular historical context.

Another change in society is that there is a growing minority of cohabitees for whom the legislation does not provide at all. The 40% of
couples who do not marry or enter into a civil partnership have no right
to claim for financial provision as the MCA 1973 simply does not
acknowledge their claims. An increasing number of family cases have to
be resolved in Chancery pursuant to the Trust of Land and Trustee Act
1996 ("TOLATA") because the parties are not married but may have
claims against each other for their respective interests in land that they
may or may not hold jointly on trust.

Such couples are treated as if they are arm's length claimants and there
is no provision for any financial support arising from the period of
cohabitation itself.

The only time a cohabitee can claim against his or her ex for maintenance is if they are dependent at the date of the other partners death
in which case a claim can be pursued under the Inheritance (Provision
for Family and Dependents) Act 1975 ("The Inheritance Act 1975").
Under the Inheritance Act 1975 it is possible to obtain maintenance
from the deceased's estate as well as a capital settlement.

Where there are children, claims can be made for a Child Maintenance
Assessment from the Child Maintenance Service whether or not the
parents are married.

It is also possible to pursue a claim pursuant to Section 15 Schedule 1
of the Children Act ("Children Act 1989") for maintenance (provided
the courts jurisdiction is available pursuant to Section 8 of the Child
Support Act 1991) and for capital and housing. These claims are for the
benefit of any child of the family and not for the benefit of the ex-
cohabitee. The ex-cohabitee loses all financial support on the day upon
which the children finish their tertiary education (at the latest).

Accordingly, we have two systems to deal with family breakdown, one
for couples in a marriage or civil partnership and a second far harsher

system for those who are not in a marriage or in a civil partnership. That second system equates with the provision given to wives in many less egalitarian societies than our own.

Whilst our system for those lucky enough to have the protection of the MCA 1973 is seen by many to be the most generous in the world another way of looking at it is that it is rather more flexible and fairer than that provided by most jurisdictions and certainly that provided for by those outside of its protection.

CHAPTER TWO
HISTORY

Contrary to what most people believe Henry VIII's divorces from Catherine of Aragon and Anne of Cleves did not open a flood gate of divorce for the rest of society in this jurisdiction.

Indeed, it was only possible to obtain a divorce by way of a private Act of Parliament. For obvious reasons this was outside of the reach of all but the extremely rich.

When parties did separate it was possible for the "innocent" wife to apply to the Ecclesiastical Courts for maintenance which was called at that time "alimony".

By the time that divorce through the civil courts was allowed by the Matrimonial Causes Act 1857 there was a body of case law upon the issue of maintenance built up by the ecclesiastical courts which required a husband to make a suitable (albeit moderate) provision for his former wife.

The Matrimonial Causes Act 1857 saw the introduction for the first time of ancillary relief by way of spousal maintenance on a discretionary basis. The court could however only order the husband to "secure" to the divorced wife such;

> "gross sum of money or such annual sum of money ……. As having regard to her fortune (if any) and to the ability of the husband and to the conduct of the party deemed reasonable".

At the time, when a woman married her property became her husband's and so very often the security needed to provide maintenance had originally come from the wife's family. During the marriage the husband would have had complete control of her property. In exchange he had an ongoing responsibility to support her even after the dissolution of the marriage.

This changed with the first Married Women's Property Act in 1870 which culminated in the Married Women's Property Act of 1882. After which a married woman could retain her own property. Following those reforms, it is not surprising that the Court of Appeal began suggesting that their discretion to provide maintenance should be "unfettered" Lister -v- Lister [1889] 15PV4 (CA).

Following the Matrimonial Causes Act 1907 the court then gained the power to order a divorced husband to make unsecured weekly or monthly payments for his wife's maintenance and support.

The One Third Rule

The method calculating a wife's maintenance based on one third of the husband's income had been used long before 1857 by the Ecclesiastical Courts. This was to provide for her lodging costs, clothing and other necessities when the couple were living separately. In cases where the wife had brought most of the capital into the marriage occasionally, she could get more than half of the available income from the secured capital. In Otway -v- Otway [1813] 2Phil 109 Mrs Otway had bought a significant capital sum into the marriage and the Judge awarded her £2,000.00 per annum (approximately £175,00.00 per annum in today's figures) from a joint income of £5,500.00 per annum (approximately £440,000.00 per annum in today's figures). As can be seen the figures are not dissimilar to what a spouse might get today albeit of course her capital remained Mr. Otway's.

In the case of Sherwood -v- Sherwood [1928] at page 215 Lord Merridale refers to an expectation that the wife would be awarded one third of the husband's income as being "axiomatic" this does not mean that a one third division was a binding rule (despite it being called one) rather it was a starting point or a guide to the court, see Stibbe -v- Stibbe [1931] P105.

Lord Denning extended this guide to the division of capital as well as the way we calculate maintenance in the case of Watchel -v- Watchel [1973] FAM72 stating:

> "a starting point of one third of the combined resources of the parties is as good and rational a starting point as any other".

The one third calculation continued to be used after the introduction of the MCA 1973. As many wives by then were working and had an income of their own one third was calculated by adding the parties' two incomes together and dividing by three. If the wife's income was less than this figure maintenance would be ordered at the sum to make up the difference. For example if the husband was earning £4,500.00 per month and the wife was earning £1,500.00 per month the total would be £6,000.00 one third of which is £2,000.00 therefore the wife would receive £500.00 per month the net effect of this is to leave the husband with 100% more income than the wife.

Meeting an applicant's reasonable requirement is another way of tackling the calculation of maintenance. In Louis -v- Louis LR I&P D 230 the wife was receiving £40.00 per annum permanent alimony from her husband's income of £120.00 per annum. She applied to vary that sum upwards when his pay increased to £480.00 per annum. She did not get awarded one third of that sum as the court applied the reasonable requirement test finding that it was more expensive for the husband to live in India where he had been posted than in England and the wife was only awarded £190.00 per annum.

The application of a reasonable requirements approach to a maintenance award is often found in cases where the courts are reluctant to provide a wife with what was perceived as too great an income. That is, an income in excess of the amount she needed to support her usual needs and standard of living.

In the case of Kettlewell -v Kettlewell [1898] P138 the joint income was £20,000.00 per annum (around £1,275,000.00 in today's money) the court awarded Mrs Kettlewell £3,000.00 per annum (equivalent to £225,000.00 per annum in today's figures) Sir HG Jean P stating that although the ordinary rule would be to allow a wife one third of the joint income an award of that size "would clearly be too much".

Following on from this decision there was a period where the courts felt bound not to award maintenance of more than £3,000.00 per annum until the Court of Appeal decided that there was no such binding rule in the case of Hulton -v- Hulton [1916] P 57.

A rather more generous definition of reasonable requirements is given by Scott LJ in the case of Ackworth -v- Ackworth [1942] P21 (LA) which he summed up as being

> "a very wide word and ...... should be read as covering everything which a wife may in reason want to do with the income which she enjoys. It includes much more than food, lodging, clothes, travelling and so on. It includes .... charity and making arrangements for the future, thus incurring various liabilities in her discretion, and it is wrong to limit it to any particular form of expenditure. The figure arrived at by the court in the first instance was not arrived at primarily on the basis of her needs. It is not for the court when making a maintenance order to decide by a close consideration of a wife's needs how much she ought to spend. I do not say that the needs of a wife should be altogether disregarded, but I do say that it is not a primary consideration".

Yet another consequence to applying a "reasonable requirement test" is the development of what became known as "the millionaires defense".

This is demonstrated in the case of Schlesinger -v- Schlesinger [1960] P191. Mr Schlesinger was found to be a man of great wealth. It was decided that he did not need to provide the court with a full discovery of his financial circumstances. It was simply accepted that he had a nominal income of £110,000.00 per annum and net capital assets of approximately £2,000,000.00 (£40,000,000.00 in today's figures) Mrs Schlesinger had no income or capital of her own and was awarded £20,000.00 per annum (equivalent to £400,000.00 per annum in today's figures).

This is one of the approaches that was challenged and discredited in 2000 in the landmark case of White -v- White [2000] UK HL54.

Cases where Joint income did not meet needs

Where there was not enough money to be shared between the parties the court would attempt to provide the husband and the wife with a comparable standard of living. Kershaw -v- Kershaw [1966] P13 and Ackworth -v- Ackworth [1942] P91. It was however the case that the husband's expenses were looked at first to reach a so called "just solution" see Chichester -v- Chichester [1936] P129.

Dum Sola Et Castra Vixerit

As we have seen in 1857 the Civil Court gained the power to make provision for wives by way of periodical payments of maintenance that was secured on capital (often the wife's capital) until 1907 when it became possible to order unsecured payments. This provision however could only be accessed by an innocent wife usually a wife abandoned following her husband's adultery. Furthermore, provision was limited to her remaining dum sola (on her own) and castra vexerit (chaste). The major reforms to the divorce legislation at the end of the 1960's which culminated in the MCA 1973 ended those prohibitions and defined spousal maintenance in Section 23 (1) (a) as an order that

> "either party to the marriage shall make to the other such periodical payments for such term as maybe specified in the order"

Section 23 (3) (a) also allowed for financial provision by way of lump sums payable to either party for

> "the purpose of enabling that other party to meet any liabilities or expenses reasonably incurred by him or her in maintaining himself or herself or any child of the family".

Section 25 of the MCA 1973 sets out the

> "matters to which the court is to have regard in deciding how to exercise its powers under Section 25"

and that by paragraph 2(g)

> "the conduct of each of the parties if that conduct is such that it would in the opinion of the court be inequitable to disregard it".

Lord Denning dealt with the issue of conduct in Watchell stating: -

> "when Parliament in 1857 introduced divorce by the Courts of Law, it based it on the doctrine of matrimonial offence. That affected all that followed if a person was the guilty party in a divorce suit it went hard with him or her. It affected so many things. The custody of the children depended on it, so did the award of maintenance to say nothing of their standing in society. So serious were the consequences that divorce suits were contested at great length and at much cost".

"where it was the wife who had caused the breakdown of the marriage either through adultery, her behaviour or desertion she could not expect support from her husband".

However, Lord Denning went on to find that: -

"in the financial adjustments consequence upon the dissolution of a marriage which has irretrievably broken down the imposition of financial penalties ought seldom to find a place".

This was a pivotable decision. Since 1973 conduct is very rarely successfully pleaded to prevent the payment of maintenance.

Long before the reforms introduced by the MCA 1973 there had been disquiet expressed by the Court of Appeal in particular about the harsh consequence of the concept of Dum Sola and Casta Vixerit and the inability of a wife held responsible for the breakdown of a marriage to have any financial support.

Prior to 1857 the Ecclesiastical Courts had ensured that even an adulterous wife should have some provision made for her. In the case of Robertson -v- Fargrossa [1883] 9PD94 (CO) the Court of Appeal spoke out as to whether or not Parliament had been correct to depart from that practice.

It went further in Ashcroft -v- Ashcroft and Roberts (1902) P270 where the husband was a moderately wealthy timber merchant. There were 5 children of the family and the marriage had lasted 23 years. After her adulterous affair with Mr Roberts the wife was left alone in poor health with no means of earning a living. She was destitute. In the first instance she had succeeding in getting an order of £1.00 per week just enough to prevent her from becoming homeless. Her husband's appeal was unsuccessful, the Court of Appeal being satisfied that the court had the power to provide a "compassionate allowance" for wives in such circumstances.

By the 1960s the concept of "compassionate allowance" was seen as insufficient to support wives in such circumstances and the Ashcroft decision was regarded as having come from a past age with no place in the contemporary law of maintenance.

Porter -v- Porter [1969] 3ER 640 was a case where the court decided that before a wife was deprived of her right to maintenance it would be for the husband to establish that her misconduct was of such

"a really serious nature, disruptive, intolerable and unforgiveable"

that it would be inequitable to disregard it. The court indicated that its discretionary powers would enable it to provide for such wife and the court commented that

"the law is a living thing moving with the times and not a creature of dead or moribund of thought".

CHAPTER THREE
THE MATRIMONIAL CAUSES
ACT 1973 ("MCA 1973")

The MCA 1973 completely reformed the law of divorce providing one ground for divorce that of irretrievable breakdown of the marriage proved on the basis of one of five facts.

It allowed for a divorce based on separation after 2 years with consent and also after 5 years with no consent. It also allowed for a divorce with the proof of adultery confined to the Respondent's confession and allowed for unreasonable behaviour to be pleaded. As well as two years desertion.

As a result, defended petitions became a rarity. It was no longer necessary to have a painful trial attributing blame to one or other of the parties for the breakdown of the marriage.

As well as the new law providing for financial provision by way of a lump sum payment it also allowed for the transfer of property pursuant to Section 24.

What it did not do was to provide for clean breaks between the parties unless the parties both consented to the same.

Section 23 allowed for maintenance payments to be made as well as lump sum payments. It did not change the way in which the courts had been deciding maintenance between the parties other than to clarify what the court would be taking into consideration pursuant to Section 25.

Section 25 also had a direction to the court at the end of it to:-

"exercise its powers to place the parties so far as it is practicable and having regard to their conduct just to do so in the financial position in which they would have been if the marriage had not broken down and each had properly discharged his or her financial obligations and responsibilities to the other".

The Judges interpreted this as maintaining the historic duty of husbands to maintain wives.

The MCA 1973 was considered to be a very radical piece of legislation. It was opposed by the church and hostility was expressed to the reforms in the press.

The idea that a wife could get a transfer of property, a lump sum and maintenance was dubbed "a meal ticket for life".

The hostility led to a Law Commissioner's report (number 112/1981) The Financial Consequences of Divorce. The results of the report led to the introduction of the Matrimonial and Family Proceedings 1984 Act. The 1984 Act amended the Matrimonial Causes Act 1973 so that the direction to the Court in Section 25 to seek to put the parties in the financial position they would have been had the marriage not failed,was abolished.

A new Section 25A was added.

Section 25A introduces a formal duty of the court to consider a clean break between the parties both when a financial order is first made and on any application for a variation and provides the court with the power to dismiss the payments without the consent of the Applicant or the Respondent. A power that it had not had prior to the introduction of this section.

Section 25A states:

"On or after the grant of a Decree of divorce ……... if the court decides to exercise its power under Section 23 (i) (a) (b) or (c) or Section 24 or Section 24A in favour of a party to the marriage it shall be the duty of the court to consider whether it would be appropriate so to exercise those powers so that the financial obligations of each party towards the other will be terminated as soon as after the grant of the decree as the court thinks just and unreasonable.

Where the court decides in such a case to make a periodical payments or secured periodical payments order in favour of a party to the marriage the court shall in particular consider whether it would be appropriate to require those payments to be made or secured only for such term as would in the opinion of the court be sufficient to enable a party in whose favour the order is made to adjust without undue hardship to determination of his or her financial dependence on the other party."

The duty to consider an early severance of financial ties applies in every case.

By section 25A (1) the duty is mandatory and applies not just to those cases where there are resources that command a lump sum payment in the expectation that it will generate unearned income for the recipient spouse thus obviating a need for maintenance but to those cases where capital is limited or non-existent resulting in a need for a maintenance order whether it be for a term order or a life time order.

This duty is replicated in similar provisions in Section 31(which allows for a variation of an order for periodical payments of maintenance) to emphasize that the duty to create a clean break applies when the court considers a variation.

The 1984 Act also introduced Section 28 (1A) providing the court with the power to make a term order which cannot be extended: -

"where a periodical payments orders or secured periodical payments order in favour of a party to a marriage is made on or after the grant of a decree of divorce or nullity (and a further amendment dissolution of a civil partnership) the court may direct that party shall not be entitled to apply under Section 31 below for the extension of the term specified in the order."

Thus, in every case where periodical payments are under consideration the court has to ask: -

- How long is maintenance required to achieve financial independence?

- Would a Term Maintenance Order impose hardship on the recipient?

- Would that hardship be undue?

- Taking into account the findings relating to the proceeding question for what is the just and reasonable duration of the liability?

- If a Term Maintenance Order is to be fixed should it be accompanied by a prohibition under Section 28 (1A)?

CHAPTER FOUR
THE STATUTE AND
THE RULES

The rules dealing with applications for periodical payments of maintenance are set out in the Family Procedure Rules 2010 ("FPR 2010").

The FPR 2010 directs the court to exercise an overriding objective which is in line with the Civil Procedure Rules. Rule 1.1 (2) directs the court to ensure it is "dealing with a case justly so far as practicable by: -

(a) ensuring that it is dealt with expeditiously

(b) dealing with the case in ways which are proportionate to the nature, importance and complexity of the issues.

(c) ensuring that the parties are on an equal footing.

(d) saving expenses

(e) allotting to it an appropriate share of the court's reasonable resources, while taking into account the need to allot resources to other cases."

In accordance with Rule 1.4 the court has a duty to actively manage cases.

Orders for Maintenance Pending Suit and periodical payments of maintenance as well as capital provision have been known as Financial Orders since the creation of the Family Courts on the 22nd April 2014. (following the enactment of the Crime and Courts Act 2013) rather than "Ancillary Relief Orders" which is now an obsolete term.

A Financial Order is obtained by applying for a financial remedy (see Rule 2.3 (1)).

Applications for periodical payments (a financial remedy) are made in the Family Court with the exception of applications made under the Inheritance Act 1975 where the High Court retains jurisdiction. This allows for an application to be made against the estate of a deceased spouse for maintenance provision. This can be particularly useful if there is a delay in the administration of an estate. It is (as previously mentioned) a remedy that is also available to cohabitees who can prove dependency at the date of death. It is not necessary for a spouse to prove dependency.

Financial Remedy is dealt with in Part (II) of the MCA 1973.

Section 21 directs the applicant who is a party to the marriage or a civil partnership in connection with divorce, nullity or judicial separation to make applications under Section 22 for Maintenance Pending Suit and Section 23 for periodical payments.

If there are no proceedings pending to terminate the relationship Section 27 can be relied upon if there is proof of neglect by one party of the other to provide reasonable maintenance.

Procedure

Part 9 of the Family Proceedings Rule 2010 (FPR 2010) deals with all applications for financial remedy in the Family Court.

The legislation to deal with financial remedy for the Magistrates sitting in the Family Court remains the Domestic Proceedings and Magistrates Court Act 1978 ("DPMA 1978") the procedure to make such an application is set out at Part 9.18 – 23 of the FPR 2010.

Applications to the magistrates are made on Form A1. A financial statement on Form E1 is filed with the court. The grounds for making such an application are: -

(i) Failure to provide reasonable maintenance.

(ii) The behaviour of the Respondent.

(iii) The desertion of the Applicant by the Respondent.

As well as making an order for Periodical payments and maintenance the Magistrates have the power to order lump sum payments of up to £1,000.00. There is also a power to make interim orders.

An application pursuant to the DPMCA 1978 is not dependent upon a petition for divorce, nullity or dissolution of a civil partnership having been issued.

Together with the provisions made under Section 27 the MCA 1973 this provides a way forwards where maintenance is an immediate need, funds are limited, and a small amount of capital is needed to make progress towards divorce. An application for a legal services order can also be issued at this stage.

Applications on Form A

An application for periodical payments pursuant to the MCA 1973 is made on Form A which includes the information indicating what if anything has been done to comply with the pre-application protocol that requires the parties to consider alternative dispute resolution.

Alternative Dispute Resolution ("ADR"); and MIAMS

The Form A requires a signed statement from a mediator to confirm that the case is not fit for mediation. The form is known as a MIAMS form. This is because the first meeting with a mediator is often called a Mediation Information and Assessment Meeting hence MIAM. Whilst every mediator that is consulted will work to try and explore the possibility of mediation with the Applicant a MIAM's meeting frequently ends the process with the completion of the certificate which appears at paragraph 4 of the Form A. Exemptions from such a meeting are set out in paragraph 3. They include cases where the Applicant has been a victim of domestic violence from the Respondent; cases where one of the parties is overseas or unable to travel to mediation and cases of urgency.

Mediation is not the only form of ADR available.

Arbitration

The parties can enter into Arbitration. The Institute of Family Law Arbitrators can be contacted at www.ifla.org.uk. Arbitration commences when the parties enter into an agreement to appoint an Arbitrator to adjudicate a dispute and make an award. The parties can decide with the Arbitrator what disclosure is needed to resolve a dispute; where a hearing will take place and when. It is a much quicker process than the issue of court proceedings and an Arbitrator can be asked to deal with periodical payments or maintenance pending suit very quickly. Once an Arbitrator is appointed the parties are bound by his or her findings and the award that they make. The order is then lodged with a draft order at the court if divorce proceedings are pending.

The procedure for lodging an arbitrator's award is set out in the case of S -v- S [2014] EWHC7 (FAM) a decision of St James Munby (P) and his practice guidance of 23rd November 2015.

If proceedings on Form A have already been issued the court will stay those proceedings to allow for an arbitration award to be made and the court will process a Consent Order reflecting an award using the same procedure to make a collaborative agreement into an order.

Collaborative Agreements

This is a process whereby the parties sign a Partnership Agreement with each other and their respective collaborative lawyers to resolve their financial proceedings through four-way meetings. If the meetings fail, then the collaborative lawyers cannot continue to act. This is due to the open nature of the meetings when both parties will need to have put their cards on the table and much of the discussions would be Without Prejudice. Throughout the jurisdiction there are pods of collaborative lawyers some of which are achieving a high rate of success. There are great advantages to the parties in using this process. The system can be used to resolve maintenance as well as capital provision.

If ADR is not being followed then upon the issue of the Form A ,a Notice on Form C will be sent to the parties or their solicitors giving directions for the filing of a detailed financial statement on Form E and the filing of a Schedule of Issues, Chronology and Questionnaire. It will also provide the parties with a date for a First Directions Appointment ("FDA") and in some courts a later hearing for a Financial Dispute Resolution Hearing ("FDR").

Costs

It is important to note that there is a no order as to costs rule which applies in financial remedy proceedings. It is set out in Rule 28.3 FPR 2010 and that is supplemented by Practice Direction 28 A. It is the case that Rule 28 1.2 provides that Parts 44 (except 44.2 (2) and (3) and

44.10 (2) and (3), 46 and 47 and Rule 458 of the Civil Procedure Rules ("CPR") apply to costs in family proceedings.

The effect of these rules is to exempt financial remedy proceedings from the usual cost rules however Rule 28 3.4 (i) specifically includes Maintenance Pending Suit; Interim Periodical Payments Orders; and Orders in respect of Legal Services or any other form of interim order for the purpose of Rule 9.7 (1) (a) (b) (c) and (e).In other words costs can be pursued for these interlocutory applications. They can also be pursued in later proceedings for enforcement.

CHAPTER FIVE
MAINTENANCE PENDING SUIT AND INTERIM PERIODICAL PAYMENTS

If the Applicant needs Maintenance Pending Suit or Interim Maintenance (as the decree nisi has already been declared) an application is made pursuant to Section 22 on Form A.

The procedure is determined by Part 9 (7) of the FPR 2010. Pursuant to Part 9 (7) if the application is made before a financial statement has been filed the application which is on Form A must be accompanied by a statement which: -

- Explains why the order is necessary.

- Gives up to date financial details of the Applicant's circumstances (see Part 9.7.(3) FPR 2010).

Unless the Respondent has already filed Form E, he or she must file a statement in response at least 7 days before the hearing. Part 9.7 (4) FPR2010. A cost order can follow if the Respondent fails to do so.

An application can be made at the same time for a Periodical Payments Order to be made at the same rate as the Maintenance Pending Suit order once decree nisi has been made and there is a similar rule for civil partnerships where a conditional order of dissolution or nullity of the civil partnership has been determined Part 9.9 FPR 2010.

There is not an abundance of case law concerning Maintenance Pending Suit due to its interim status and the costs of appeal. Accordingly, what cases there are tend to be in connection with cases that have become very long and drawn out due to jurisdictional issues. There are however some principles to be taken from the following cases.

S -v- M (2012) or ER (D) 1750 (NOV) this case concerned a marriage that had only lasted one year. The Applicant wife had been served with a notice to quit by her father in law from a property that she was occupying which belonged to a company in which her father in law was the principle shareholder.

When she applied for Maintenance Pending Suit the case was built on the argument that the husband's family had significant wealth and that they were supporting the husband financially and the husband should therefore support her. The husband's defense was he had no income or assets of his own.

At first instance there was a hearing which lasted for 30 minutes where the District Judge granted the wife's application and ordered the husband to pay the wife £750.00 per month for her property expenses and £2,400.00 per month to her solicitors on account of her costs.

At a second hearing another District Judge granted the wife a freezing injunction in respect of 6 bank accounts held by the husband. The husband appealed claiming he had no money.

The case came before Coleridge J he allowed the appeal because he considered that the time estimate had been too short to hear the evidence. There was a significant difference in the evidence of the two parties and he found that there had not been time to establish the extent to which the husband's family was supporting the husband and the extent that the husband had supported the wife.

He considered the principles relevant to an MPS hearing as set out in TL -v- ML [2005] EWHC 2860 (FAM). A case where a third party had been financially supporting the husband and a Maintenance Pending Suit had been awarded however, he found that this case could be distinguished because there needed to be a finding that the third party was continuing with support and the father had given clear evidence that he was no longer providing for his son.

This is a difficult case for the practitioner as Maintenance Pending Suit is needed quickly and a longer hearing time given the capacity of the courts would push the date of the hearing back until after the First Directions Appointment or possibly even the Financial Dispute Resolution Appointment.

It is however possible to arbitrate discreet issues and consideration could be given to using an Arbitrator to deal with Maintenance Pending Suit and Interim Provision.

In MT -v- T [2013] EWHC 2001 the wife had been granted Maintenance Pending Suit of £25,000.00 per annum which by the time of the hearing with the cost orders that she had also received amounted to £900,000.00. The argument before Charles J was as to the jurisdiction of the court as the husband maintained throughout proceedings that the parties were not married. He was eventually successful after 10 years of litigation it was found that he was not married to the wife and therefore she had no claim.

Charles J expressed concern that the rules did not allow for the repayment of Maintenance Pending Suite he also commented that payments on account of costs are payments on account and should be taken into account at the time of the final Financial Remedy Order. As well as the courts exercising caution where there are jurisdictional issues Charles J's comments also impact where there is a Legal Services Order.

Such caution was demonstrated by Mostyn J in the cases of DC -v- MC (Maintenance Pending Suit) [2014] EWHC703 and MET -v- HAT (2) (2014) EWHC 717 which were both cases where there were jurisdictional issues. Both applicants were awarded MPS but at significantly less generous rates than they had been seeking.

A case that emphasises the need to demonstrate why maintenance is sought is BD -v- FD (Maintenance) [2014] EWHC4443 where an Applicant failed to obtain maintenance because Moylan J did not consider that her claims arose from her needs. It is important to establish this in an MPS application.

Legal Services Orders

Sections ss.22ZA and 22ZB MCA 1973 and the corresponding amendments to Schedule 5 to the Civil Partnership Act provide for an order or orders requiring one party to the marriage or civil partnership to pay the other an amount for the purpose of enabling the Applicant to obtain Legal Services for the purposes of the proceedings.

A Legal Services Order (LASPO) is a relief in its own right and furthermore Section 24 A(1) MCA 1973 has been amended so that the LASPO can be backed with an interim order for the sale of property. The amendments were introduced by Sections 49-50 of the Legal Aid Sentencing and Punishment of Offenders Act 2012 (LASPO) in April 2013.

Section 22ZA(b) also provides that the payments may be made in instalments that is by way of a global lump sum.

Whilst an LASPO is a separate relief and an application is made on Form D11 it can be made at the same time as an application for MPS or an order pursuant to section 27. The two applications can be heard together and a costs order can be pursued see Rule 28.3.4 (i).

Prior to the introduction of the amendments made by LASPO in April 2013 it was possible to make an application for provision for costs, within an application for MPS. The test for making such provision was:-

(a) Reasonableness;

(b) Affording each party, the opportunity to present their case on an equal footing;

(c) Was it unreasonable for the Applicant to give security against his or her assets.

The Applicant needed to demonstrate:-

(i) They had few or no assets

(ii) They could not raise a litigation loan provided by producing at least two letters from two banks refusing to lend the money.

(iii) That their solicitor would not enter into a Sears Tooth Agreement (such an agreement being one where the Applicant agrees with his or her solicitor that outstanding costs will be deducted from their assets at the end of the case).

(iv) There was no exceptionality case.

See:

- Currey -v- Currey (no.2) [2006] EWCA CIV1158;

- A-v- A (Maintenance Pending Suit provision for Legal Services [2011] 1FLR377 HolmanJ

- TL -v- ML and others (Ancillary Relief: Claims against assets of extended family) [2005] EWH 2860 (Fam) Mr Nicholas Mostyn (as he then was); and

- Re G (Maintenance Pending Suit) [2006] EWHC 1834 (FAM) Munby J (as he then was).

Since the introduction of the LASPO provisions the court may not make an order unless it is satisfied that without the amount sought for costs the Applicant would not "reasonably" be able to obtain "appropriate" Legal Services for the proceedings or part of the proceedings.

In the case of AM-v-SS [2014] EWHC 865 Moylan J (as he then was) had to consider an application for a Legal Services Order where the level of the husband's wealth was being vigorously challenged by the Applicant. The husband was defending that challenge by claiming the wealth was really his family's and not his. The Judge found that in such cases the object was to ensure that the parties were on an equal footing in the proceedings. He found that the court could make "robust assumptions" about the husband's ability to pay legal fees. He provided the wife with a £150,000.00 charge against the property owned by the husband for legal fees and imposed an order preventing the husband from selling the property or increasing his own mortgage.

Section 22ZA(4) still requires an Applicant to show that they cannot obtain a loan or secure a charge against their property to do so.

Section 22ZB sets out the matters that the court must give regard by codifying the principles set out above in Currey -v- Currey.

Pursuant to Section 22ZB the court must have regard to: -

a) Both parties' financial resources.

b) Both parties' needs.

c) The subject matter of the proceedings.

d) Whether the Respondent is legally represented.

e) The Applicant's litigation conduct in the proceedings including his or her approach to mediation.

f) Any outstanding costs order owed by the Applicant to the Respondent.

g) Any hardship which would be caused to the Respondent by the making of the order.

h) The ability of the Respondent to continue to pay for his or her Legal Services if an order is to be made.

In BN -v- MA [2013] EWHC4250 (FAM) Mostyn J, an Applicant failed to get a Legal Services Order because she wanted to challenge a pre-marital Agreement which had been unfairly negotiated. Mostyn J found that her application on Form A was "extremely speculative" "border line irresponsible" and that her "prospects of success are questionable" he also found that loans albeit with steep interest payments were available and that the Applicant had not provided a detailed schedule of costs.

In Rubin-v- Rubin [2014] EWHC 611 (FAM) Mostyn J provides a helpful summary of how and when to proceed with an application at paragraph 13: -

(i) "when considering the overall merits of the application for a LASPO the court is required to have regard to all the matters mentioned in Section 22ZB (1) - (3)

(ii) Without derogating from that requirement, the ability of the Respondent to pay should be judged by reference to the principles summarised in TL -v- ML [2005] EWHC 286 (FAM) [2006] 1FCR465 [2006] 1FLR1263 at Paragraph 124 (iv) and (v) where it was stated;

> "(iv) where the Affidavit or Form E disclosure by the payer is obviously deficient the court should not hesitate to make robust assumptions about his ability to pay. The court is not confined to the mere say so of the payer as to

the extent of his income or resources. In such a situation the court should err in favour of the payee.

v) Where the paying party has historically been supported through the bounty of an outsider, and where the payer is asserting that the bounty had been curtailed but where the position of the outsider is ambiguous or unclear then the court is justified in assuming that the third party will continue to supply the bounty, at least until final trial"

(iii) Where the claim for substantive relief appears doubtful, whether by virtue of a challenge to the jurisdiction or otherwise having regard to its subject matter, the court should judge the application with caution. The more doubtful it is the more cautious it should be.

(iv) The court cannot make an order unless it is satisfied that without the payment the Applicant would not reasonably be able to obtain appropriate Legal Services for the proceedings. Therefore, the exercise essentially looks to the future. It is important that the jurisdiction is not used to outflank or supplant the powers and principles governing an award of costs in CPR Part 44. It is not a surrogate inter partes costs jurisdiction. Thus, a LASPO should only be awarded to cover historical unpaid costs where the court is satisfied that without such a payment the Applicant will not reasonably be able to obtain in the future appropriately good services for the proceedings.

(v) In determining whether the Applicant can reasonably obtain funding from another source the court would be unlikely to expect her to sell or charge her home or to deplete a modest fund of savings.

This aspect is however highly fact – specific. If the home is of such a value that it appears likely that it will be sold at the conclusion of proceedings, then it may well be reasonable to expect the Applicant to charge her interest in it.

(vi) Evidence of refusals by two commercial lenders of repute will normally dispose of any issue under Section 22 ZA (4) (a) whether a litigation loan is or is not available.

(vii) In determining under Section 22 ZA (4) (b) whether a Sears Tooth arrangement can be entered into a statement of refusal by the Applicant solicitors should normally answer the question.

(viii) If a litigation loan is offered at a very high rate of interest it would be unlikely to be reasonable to expect the Applicant to take it unless the Respondent offered an undertaking to meet that interest, the court later considering it just so to order.

(ix) The order should normally contain an undertaking by the Applicant that she will repay to the Respondent such part of the amount ordered if and to the extent that the court is of the opinion when considering costs at the conclusion of the proceedings that she ought to do so. If such an undertaking is refused the court will want to think twice before making the order.

(x) The court should make clear in its ruling or judgement which of the legal services mentioned in Section 22 ZA (10) the payment is for; it is not however necessary to spell this out in the order. A LASPO may be made for the purposes, in particular of advice and assistance in the form of representation and any form of dispute resolution, including mediation. Thus, the power may be exercised before any financial remedy proceedings have been commenced in order to finance any form of alternative dispute resolution, which plainly would include arbitration proceedings.

(xi) Generally speaking the court should not fund the Applicant beyond the FDR but the court should readily grant a hearing date for further funding to be fixed shortly after the FDR. This is a better course than ordering a sum for the whole proceedings of which part is deferred under Section 22 ZA (7). The court will be better placed to assess accurately the true costs of taking the matter to trial after a failed FDR when the final hearing is relatively imminent and the issues to be tried are more clearly defined.

(xii) When ordering costs funding for a specific period, monthly instalments are to be preferred to a single lump sum payment. It is true that a single payment avoids anxiety on the part of the Applicant as to whether the monthly sums will actually be paid as well as the annoyance inflicted on the Respondent in having to make monthly payments. However, monthly payments more accurately reflect what would happen if the Applicant were paying her lawyers from her own resources, and very likely will mirror the position of the Respondent. If both sets of lawyers are having their fees met monthly this puts them on an equal footing both in the conduct of the case and in any dialogue about settlement. Further, monthly payments are more readily susceptible to variation under Section 22 ZA (8) should circumstances change.

(xiii) If the application for a LASPO seeks an award including the costs of that very application the court should bear in mind Section 22 ZA (9) whereby a party's bill of costs in assessment proceedings is treated as reduced by the amount of any LASPO made in his or her favour. Thus, if a LASPO is made in an amount which includes the anticipated costs of that very application for the LASPO then an order for costs of that application will not bite save to the extent that the actual costs of the application may exceed such part of the LASPO as is referable thereto.

(xiv) A LASPO is designated as an interim order and is to be made under Part 18 Procedure (see FPR rules 9.7 (1) (da) (2)). Fourteen days' notice must be given (see FPR Rules 18.8 (b) (i) and PD9A para 12.1) .The application must be supported by written evidence (see FPR Rule 18.8 (2) That evidence must not only address the matters in ss22ZB(1)-(3) but must include a detailed estimate of the costs both incurred and to be incurred. If the application seeks a hearing sooner than 14 days from the date of issue of the application pursuant to FPR Rule 18.8 (4) then the written evidence in support must explain why it is fair and just that the time should be abridged".

CHAPTER SIX

APPLICATIONS PURSUANT TO SECTION 23 MATRIMONIAL CAUSES ACT 1973 FOR PERIODICAL PAYMENTS OF MAINTENANCE

All applications under Section 23 MCA 73 are considered in the light of the matters that the court must take into regard which are set out in Section 25 of the Matrimonial Causes Act 1973 as follows: -

1. It shall be the duty of the court in deciding whether to exercise its powers under Section 23 …. to have regard to all the circumstances of the case, first consideration being given to the welfare while a minor of any child of the family who has not attained the age of 18.

2. …… the court shall in particular have regard to the following matters: -

    a. The income, earning capacity, property and other financial resources which each of the parties to the marriage has or is likely to have in the foreseeable future, including in the case of earning capacity any increase in that capacity it would in the opinion of the court be reasonable to expect a party to the marriage to take steps to acquire.

    b. The financial needs, obligations and responsibilities which each of the parties to the marriage has or is likely to have in the foreseeable future.

c. The standard of living enjoyed by the family before the breakdown of the marriage.

d. The age of each party to the marriage and the duration of the marriage.

e. Any physical or mental disability of either of the parties to the marriage.

f. The contributions which each of the parties has made or is likely to make to the wellbeing of the family including any contribution by looking after the home or caring for the family.

g. The conduct of each of the parties if that conduct is such that it would be in the opinion of the court in equitable to disregard it.

h. In the case of proceedings for divorce or nullity of marriage the value to each of the parties to the marriage and the benefit which by reason of the illusional annulment of the marriage that party will lose the chance of acquiring.

Section 25 is at the heart of all proceedings for financial relief. It provides the court's discretion. It was drafted in such a way that has allowed for the courts to adapt to the enormous changes in society since 1973 but its width and breadth also explains the different strands of interpretation which can cause outrage. It is however perfectly suited to the need to treat each and every family that comes before the Family court as having its uniqueness taken into consideration.

Section 23 does not specify any particular purpose for periodical payments of maintenance. They are one of the orders available to the court to achieve its objective of fairness between the parties.

An application for periodical payments can commence on the issue of the petition (Section 26 MCA 1973) and an order can be back-dated to that date and last until the death; remarriage of the recipient or further order.

An application to vary a periodical payments order is made pursuant to Section 31MCA 1973.The order to vary can be backdated to the date of the application which is made on a Form A1. The financial evidence is disclosed on a Form E1.

Lump Sum Settlements in lieu of maintenance

During the 1990's the courts showed a marked reluctance to make clean breaks particularly if: -

(i)   There were minor children living with the payee.

(ii) The payee was over 50.

(iii) The payee had a disability (e.g. asthma).

But running parallel to these decisions there was a trend in so called "big money" cases to provide the payee (invariably the wife) with a lump sum to meet needs (including a house) generously interpreted. The lump sum would be calculated by consulting actuarial tables first used in the Duxbury case. These tables are referred to as Duxbury Tables (Duxbury -v- Duxbury [1981] 1FLR 7).

This resulted in the very wealthy payer hiding behind a "millionaires defense" as long as they he could prove the affordability of the lump sum.

This practice came to a holt when the House of Lords decided the case of White -v- White [2001] 1AC596 2FLR 981.

The decision in the White case appears on first reading to relate more to capital provision than to that of maintenance. In this case their Lordships find that when dividing the capital held by the parties to the marriage a theoretical "yard stick of equality" should be considered and the court should start by dividing the parties' matrimonial assets equally.

This was the first time that their Lordships had considered an appeal concerning financial provision following the major changes to divorce introduced by the MCA 1973. Accordingly, they attempted to provide a blue print for future applications. The idea that a wife's share of the assets could be limited to providing her with a lump sum to meet her reasonable needs was outlawed.

The lead judge Lord Nichols of Birkenhead stating in the later decision of Miller -v- Miller: McFarlane -v- McFarlane [2006] UKHL 24

> "For many years one principle applied by the courts was to have regard to the reasonable requirements of the claimant, usually the wife, and treat this as a determinative of the extent of the claimant's award. Fairness lay in enabling the wife to continue to live in the fashion to which she had become accustomed. The glass ceiling first put in place was shattered by the decision of your Lordships House in the White case"

In summary Mrs White regarded herself as her husband's business partner. During the marriage she had helped him run the family farm. At first instance she was given a lump sum based on her needs. What she wanted was a settlement to enable her to continue farming. The case is relevant for the issue of maintenance due to the outlawing of lump sums to meet needs only. It commenced a trend for what came to be seen by the press and other critics as exceptionally generous awards to payees.

Following the White decision in 2003 the Court of Appeal dealt with the case of Fleming -v- Fleming (2003) EWCA CIV 1841; [2004] 1FLR667.

It concerned an application by the wife to extend a term maintenance order made on the 15th December 1998 which was due to end on the 20th December 2002. The order did not include a Section 28 (1) (A) bar.

No one had any idea at the time of the variation how the 14-year order has come about.

It was the case that by the time of the application Mrs Fleming lived with another man. She was working part time as a dentist; she and her partner could manage on their joint income and were not obliged to use any of their capital to maintain a reasonable standard of living.

At first instance before a circuit judge Mrs Fleming's maintenance was reduced from £1,000.00 per month to £500.00 per month but the order was extended to a life time order.

The Court of Appeal found that the judge was under an obligation to consider whether it was appropriate to terminate the periodical payments order provided the outcome could be achieved without undue hardship to the wife. Because the judge had found that the wife had some working capacity despite suffering from a disability and that she was managing her finances with her new partner it followed that it was illogical to extend the maintenance as this did not fit in with the judge's findings.

"..... the Judge exercising the power to vary under Section 31 holds both a duty to terminate if achievable without undue hardship and also power to do so by making a lump sum order in substitute for continuing periodical payments. Those obligations are much enhanced in any case where there has been a previous

term ordered. The undoubted intention of the parties and the court in December 1988 was that the payer's obligations would terminate absolutely on the 1st December 2002. In such circumstances the exercise of a power to extend obligations requires some exceptional justification"
– per Lord Justice Thorpe.

These findings have caused considerable debate amongst the judiciary and as we shall see they have been challenged particularly by the Family Division.

Despite the judicial challenges, the decision in the Fleming case is a Court of Appeal decision and it has subsequently been approved of by the House of Lords in the McFarlane case, thus for the practitioner until it is overturned by the Supreme Court when making an application to extend a term order evidence of exceptional circumstances should be pleaded where it exists.

CHAPTER SEVEN
THE CLEAN BREAK PROBLEM

When the 1984 Act amendments were first introduced there were a flurry of applications to terminate periodical payments of maintenance by way of a clean break but after a short period of time the courts began to show an increasing reluctance to find that the payee could adjust to the loss of maintenance.

Flavell -v- Flavell [1997] 1FLR353

In this case a District Judge made an initial order for periodical payments at the rate of £450.00 per month for 2 years. The husband's application for there to be a ban on an extension pursuant to Section 28 (1) (A) was refused.

The wife applied to vary and extend the order (before the 2 years had expired). The District Judge gave her a 6 months extension with a bar on further extensions. On appeal the limitation on the term was removed but the order was reduced to £250.00 per month.

The case went on to the Court of Appeal where clarification was provided as to the powers of the court pursuant to Section 31.

They found that the power to vary orders pursuant to Section 31 (1) MCA 1973 is unrestricted. It is not dependent upon exceptional circumstances or material change which are merely matters which could affect the court's discretion. On every application to vary an order the court should look at the matter "de novo" Furthermore the Court of Appeal confirmed that the amendments to the 1973 Act proposed no more than an aspiration that the parties should be self-sufficient and the power to determine dependency should be exercised only if the adjustment could be made without undue hardship.

They went on to find that it was not usually appropriate to terminate periodical payments for a wife in her mid-50's unless she had substantial capital or a significant earning capacity. They found that the risk of ill health and loss of employment were real factors to be taken into account and that the optimism of the district judge at the time of the original order that the wife could become self-sufficient had not been born out and it was wholly unacceptable on the facts that he had found to dismiss the term order.

The Court of Appeal also spoke out against prohibiting an extension in the case of Waterman -v- Waterman [1989] FLR380. In that case the judge at first instance had provided the wife who had care of the parties five-year-old child an order for 5 years with a Section 28 (1) (A) bar. The marriage itself had only lasted 17 months. Whilst they agreed that the judge was fully entitled to form the view that there should have been a term order, they found that the imposition of the Section 28 (1) (A) bar was "plainly wrong" and Sir Steven Brown P commented as follows: -

> "He does not appear to me to have given proper consideration to the real uncertainty as to the future of this particular wife. I believe that he was fully entitled on the evidence before him to express his view that there was still a child of tender years and to the uncertainty as to what the position might be in 5 years' time, he was wrong to add a prohibition preventing her from applying for an extension under any circumstances."

Another case where the Court of Appeal criticised the termination of a life time order by a Circuit Judge on appeal from a District Judge is Barrett -v- Barrett 1988 2FLR 51672. Even though the wife had been awarded most of the capital in the marriage the lifetime order was restored. Butler Sloss LJ considered that too much emphasis had been put on termination: -

"in my judgment the learned Judge was fettering himself by saying that he was obliged to look upon this approach as a priority and he did not in my judgment direct himself correctly on the way in which he should approach this matter … that is to say take all aspects of Section 25 and Section 25 A into consideration, look at them and in the circumstances of the particular case come to a conclusion whether it be right that this wife should have termination of her periodical payments after the expiry of four years. I do not see Parliament taking from the Court the exercise of discretion in the widest possible way so long as each aspect of Section 25 so far as appropriate and Section 25 (A) particularly sub section (1) are clearly in the mind of the court and are given appropriate weight to the particular case which is before the court. For my part I take the view that the learned Judge misdirected himself in his overall approach to the consideration of periodical payments for wives".

In the case of Clutton -v- Clutton [1991] 1FLR 242 where the wife wanted all the equity in the matrimonial home and no maintenance, she was instead given a lifetime order and the matrimonial home was transferred to her with a chargeback in the sum of £7,000.00 to the husband. When the husband appealed the charge was converted to a Mesher Order, but the wife's lifetime maintenance stayed in place.

Thus, we have a pattern established by the 1990's of the courts showing reluctance to make a clean break; unless capital was available to provide the same.

In C -v- C [1997] 2FLR26 there had been a 9-month marriage, but the wife got periodical payments for life as there was a young child. Ward LJ commenting that in such cases: -

"the first task is to consider a clean break which pursuant to Section 25 (1) (A) requires the court to consider whether it would be appropriate to exercise its power so that the financial obligations of each party with the other will be terminated as soon after the grant of the decree as the court considers just and reasonable. If there is no clean break and a periodical payments order is to be made the court must decide pursuant to Section 25 what amount is to be ordered. The duration of the marriage is a factor relevant to the determination of quantum. If a periodical payments order is made whether for 5p per annum or whatever; the question is whether it would be appropriate to impose a term because in the absence of such a direction the order will endure for joint lives or until the remarriage of the payee see Section 28 (1) (A.) The test is this; is it appropriate to order periodical payments only for such term as in the opinion of the court would be sufficient to enable the payee to adjust without undue hardship to the determination of financial dependence on the paying party? What is appropriate must of necessity depend on all the circumstances of the case, including the welfare of any minor child, on the Section 25 checklist factors, one of which is the duration of the marriage. It is however not appropriate simply to say: -

"this is a short marriage therefore a term must be imposed".

Financial dependency being evident from the very making of an order for periodical payments the question is whether in light of all the circumstances of the case the payee can adjust and adjust without undue hardship to the determination of financial dependence and if so when. The question is can she adjust not should she adjust. In answering that question the court will pay attention not only to the duration of the marriage but to the effect the marriage and its breakdown and the need to care for any minor children had and will continue to have on the earning capacity of the payee and the extent to which she is no longer in the position she would have been but for the marriage, its con-sequences and its breakdown. It is highly material to consider any difficulties the payee may have in entering or re-entering the labour market, resuming a fractured career and making up any lost ground. The courts cannot form its opinion that a term is appropriate without evidence to support its conclusion. Facts supported by evidence must therefore justify a reasonable expectation that the payee can and will become self-sufficient. Gazing into the crystal ball does not give rise to such a reasonable expectation. Hope, with or without pious exhortations to end dependency is not enough".

He went onto say;

"it is necessary for the court to form an opinion not only that the payee will adjust but also the payee will have adjusted within the term that is fixed. The court may be in a position of such certainty that it can impose a deferred clean break by prohibiting an extension of the term pursuant to Section 28 (1) (A) if however, there is doubt whether and when self-sufficiency will be attained it is wrong to require the payee to extend the term. If there is uncertainty about the appropriate length of term the proper call is to impose no term but leave the payer to seek the variation and if necessary, go through the same exercise this time pursuant to Section 31 (7) (a)"

These findings were reinforced again in G -v- G (1997) 1FLR 368 where the court did not consider a term order ought to have been made in respect of a wife who was then aged 43 after a twenty-year marriage. Unfortunately, a term order had been made until her daughter attained the age of 18 years. One month after her daughter's birthday she applied to vary the order her application failed because the court cannot resurrect an order that has terminated.

When the matter came before the Court of Appeal that decision was upheld however the court went on to express doubt (per Ward LJ): -

"whether or not it was truly appropriate to limit the petitioner's entitlement to periodical payments for five years or at all"

And further commented that; -

> "those agreeing and those making these term orders have a duty pursuant to section 25(2) to consider whether the payee can adjust"

To summarize during the 1990's it became increasingly difficult to obtain a clean break and as we shall see the decision in the Fleming case made it even more difficult.

Miller -v- Miller. McFarlane -v McFarlane [2006] 1FLR1186

The second time a financial provision order was considered by the House of Lords was in 2006 when the cases of Miller and McFarlane were heard.

Following the decision in the White case there had been a flurry of litigation primarily around the issues of contribution and the division of capital. The Miller case concerned the court's decision to provide a wife in a very short marriage with a settlement of approximately £5 million from a £17 million pot. The husband's appeal was dismissed.

What was of more significance with respect to the issue of maintenance is the decision in the McFarlane case.

Mrs McFarlane had practiced in the city as a solicitor before the parties had their second child. Mr McFarlane was an accountant. At the time that Mrs McFarlane retired from practice she was earning a similar amount to her husband. Their marriage had lasted 16 years when they separated. By the time of separation Mr McFarlane was earning about £753,000.00 per annum net. It was agreed that they had insufficient capital to create a clean break (they had assets of circa £3 million).

At first instance Mrs. McFarlane was awarded a life time maintenance order of £250,0000.00 per annum. Mr. McFarlane appealed. On appeal a High Court Judge reduced the amount to £180,000.00 per annum.

On appeal to the Court of Appeal the sum of £250,000.00 per annum was reinstated but on a five-year term maintenance order.

Mrs. McFarlane appealed, and she was successful the district judge's original order was reinstated. In reaching this conclusion their Lordships found that periodical payments could be ordered to meet compensation in Mrs McFarlane's case for the loss of her career as a city solicitor. There was also consideration given, primarily by Baroness Hale that her application for maintenance could also achieve sharing as well as needs. Furthermore, at paragraph 97 Lord Nichols and at paragraph 155 Lady Hale accepted the findings of Lord Thorpe in Fleming. That is that an extension of a term order requires some "exceptional justification" they then decided that the burden of obtaining a variation of maintenance should be borne by Mr McFarlane who could apply for a variation downwards pursuant to Section 31 in the future. Lord Nichols justification for the order for the purpose of affording compensation as well as meeting needs is as follows;

> "….. if one party's earning capacity has been damaged at the expense of the other party during the marriage it would be extraordinary if where necessary the court could not order the advantaged party to pay compensation to the other out of his enhanced earnings. It would be most unfair if the absence of capital assets were regarded as cancelling his obligation to pay compensation in respect of the continuing economic advantage he has obtained from the marriage".

Baroness Hale went even further. She identified not only compensation for marriage related "financial disadvantage" as a ground upon which to make an order for periodical payments in excess of the wife's reasonable requirements but specified as follows: -

> "the main family asset is the husband's very substantial earning power generated over a lengthy marriage in which the couple deliberately chose that the wife should devote herself to home and family and the husband to work and to have a career. The wife is undoubtably entitled to generous income provision for herself and for the sake of their children including sums which will enable her to provide for her old age and to insure the husband's life. She is also entitled to a surplus on the principles both of sharing the fruits of the marriage partnership and of compensation for the comparable she might have been in had she not compromised her own career for the sake of them all. The fact that she wanted to do so is neither here nor there".

The aftermath of this decision was that it became more difficult to obtain a clean break settlement even in the "big money cases".

The Flavell decision had established that a wife who is a primary carer of children and unable to work is likely to require a joint lives order notwithstanding Section 25 (A). It also established that it is not usually appropriate to provide for the termination of periodical payments where a wife is in her mid-50's unless she has substantive capital and a significant earning capacity.

C -v- C established that if there is uncertainty it is better to make a life time order and leave it to the payer to apply for a variation.

Added to this is the House of Lords decision to introduce the concept providing compensation: -

> "aimed at redressing any significant prospective economic disparity between the parties arising from the way they conducted their marriage"

albeit there was early recognition that it is only available if there are insufficient assets to provide the same, and their finding that the threshold established in the case of Fleming to extend the term order is so high.

The McFarlane decision provides that it is safer to make a life time order and place the burden of applying for a variation to change a maintenance order or terminate it on the payer as well as introducing the concepts of compensation and sharing.

What followed however were an increasing number of decisions at Family Division level which tried to distinguish this position.

In RP -v- RP [2007] 1FLR 2105 Coleridge J objected to the adduction of evidence concerning the wife's potential career had it been pursued with a compensation claim stating: -

> "once again a high profile case (Miller; McFarlane) heard at the highest level sends seismic reverberations throughout the whole system; touching every district registry and lawyers office in the land and even though it is a big money case and so in theory within a minute proportion of the overall case load in this field and of limited application, Pandora can be heard rattling her keys as every line of the decision is subject to scrutiny by microscope for innovative arguments and approach. Another very undesirable consequence is that clean breaks seem to be becoming more difficult to achieve, despite the statutory imperative to achieve one where reasonably possible. As claimants attempt to build up their entitlement by aggregation. This was potentially one such case".

Ironically in 2009 Mrs McFarlane was the one to apply for a variation. She did so when Mr McFarlane's income increased from £750,000.00 per annum to £1.1 million per annum. Her application for an increase came before Charles J.

Charles J commented with considerable force that it was all very well for their Lordships to impose "compensation" as a concept but not helpful when they did not provide guidance as to how quantify it. He decided that it would be incorrect to treat it like a damage claim and that he still had a statutory duty to move the parties to a clean break saying: -

> "the plans and expectations of the parties when deciding that the wife should give up her career point strongly towards the conclusion that the relevant provisions to be made for the wife from the husband's earnings should be on or before his retirement. If this is practicable and fairly done."

He determined that Mrs. McFarlane would receive 40% of Mr McFarlane's income to £750,000.00 (£300,000.00) 20% to £1 million (a further £50,000.00 and 10% of earnings over £1 million) that is a total of £360,000.00 per annum based on Mr. McFarlane's income of £1.1 million however this was converted into a term order until the 31st May 2015 when Mr McFarlane would have reached 55 years of age.

Charles J made it clear that Mrs. McFarlane was being sufficiently well paid by way of periodical payments to save a sufficient lump sum for a Duxbury type figure to give her an income of £120,000.00 per annum following the end of the order. In other words, part of the maintenance being provided for her was to create her own annuity.

He also made it clear that he did not think she would succeed in obtaining an extension of the term order given the amount of monies that he was awarding her.

What is extraordinary is that at paragraph 104 he states that: -

> "the test for the approach decided or applied in Fleming does not survive".

Furthermore, he stated that if

> "if the choice is between an extended term and a joint lives order is finally balanced the statutory steer should mitigate in favour of the former".

Mrs McFarlane did not appeal.

To summarise, the courts have not looked with favour on the concepts of compensation and sharing since the decision in McFarlane however the House of Lords have determined that "the wife's financial needs or her "reasonable requirements" are now no more of a determinative or limiting factor on the application for a periodical payments order as they are on an application for a lump sum" per Nichols LJ.

In summary there are three identifiable grounds upon which an application might be pursued;

- Needs

- Sharing and

- Compensation.

CHAPTER EIGHT
THE PROBLEMS SURROUNDING
SHARING THE PAYERS INCOME

In VB -v- JP [2008] 1FLR 742 Sir Mark Potter P then President of the Family Division said that: -

"On exit from the marriage the partnership ends and in ordinary circumstances the wife has no right or expectation of economic parity (sharing) unless and to the extent that consideration of her needs or compensation for relationship generated disadvantage so require".

In the case of B-v-S (Financial Remedy: Marital Property Regime) [2012] EWHC 265 Mostyn J was dealing with a wife who had claimed a financial remedy from the husband on a sharing basis. Both parties were foreign nationals who had lived in England since 2004 and the case dealt with difficult issues surrounding separate property regimes and post marriage settlement.

The wife sought to retain assets which were in her sole name; a lump sum of £3 million; a joint lives periodical payment order of £175,000.00 per annum and £7,500.00 per annum for each of the two children of the family.

The wife was also seeking a school fees order whereas the husband was asserting that assets should lie where they fell in accordance with the agreements that they had already reached. He offered the wife periodical payments of maintenance of £100,000.00 per annum with no periodical payments for the children as his case was that the children shared residence with each party and therefore each party should be responsible for their costs. He was happy to pay school fees.

In dealing with the matter the judge was highly critical of the sharing principle set out in McFarlane stating;

> "the reason the sharing principle is sometimes advocated as being applicable to a periodical payments claim is to reflect the theory that post-separation earnings derive from an earning capacity built up during the marriage which is in some intangible way a piece of matrimonial property there to be equitably or fairly shared. The high point of that theory is the dictum of Lady Hale as a theory it is problematic, because at the end of the day the only reason there is income and separation are because of work done after separation. A footballer who earns £100,000.00 per week earns that because he is on the pitch playing football. Certainly, the skills he was born with and the development of those skills (which may have happened during his marriage) are all reasons why he cannot command his salary, but he will not get paid it unless he plays football. The footballer has to fill the unforgiving minute with 60 seconds worth of distance from after the marriage".

The wife's settlement was determined on need with an instalment plan for the lump sums that were awarded.

The wife was to receive £1 million 18 months after the order was made, that is on the 1st June 2013, a further £1 million on the 1st June 2104 and £1,344,000.00 on 1st June 2015. She was initially to receive maintenance of £10,000.00 per month reducing to £7,500.00 on the payment of the first £1 million and then reducing to £4,300.00 on the next instalment. Her maintenance was to terminate on the payment of the balancing figure on the 1st June 2015.

In G -v- G [2012] EWHC 167 Charles J found that, a fair outcome;

> "i) is not met by an approach that seeks to achieve a dependence for life (or until re-marriage) for the payee spouse to fund a life-style equivalent to that enjoyed during the marriage.... but

ii) is met by an approach that the aim is independence and self-sufficiency based on all the financial resources that are available to the parties. From that it follows that:

iii) generally, the marital partnership does not survive as a basis for the sharing of future resources"

Albeit he does then recognize a list of exceptions to this finding which reflect the section 25 criteria. See paragraph 136.

It is however clear that there are cases where sharing has to take place as in the case of. V -v- V [2005]2FLR 697.

In this case Coleridge J made the following observations with respect to the way in which income generated by an optician's business that was being retained by the husband should be dealt with where there were insufficient assets to create a clean break and confirmed: -

"the income from SS Limited is on one view the most valuable asset in this case. It has been acquired following a very long marriage and as I have indicated it is part of a continuum so far as the generation of income from such a source is concerned. I ask myself the question; is it fair in those circumstances for this husband or indeed a husband in similar circumstances to be left with double the wife's disposable income in circumstances where it is not suggested that there should be a clean break? The net effect of the district judge's current division is that as he has set out the wife receives one third of the net income the husband two thirds ergo 100% more than the wife. There is almost no guidance or authority in relation to the way in which the court should determine this aspect of an ancillary relief claim save in circumstances where the incomes are huge. They provide no assistance to me whatever. This is not such a case. This is a case where there was a solid secure income which is capable of providing decently for both sides although obviously after division will lead to a considerable drawing-in of horns by both husband and wife. Again, there can of course be no hard and fast rules in these cases particularly in relation to the division of available income – Section 25 are the only real criteria.

In my judgment she should have 40% of the income and the husband 50%"

40% also seems to be an attractive percentage or share where there is an income being accumulated over a very short period of time by the payer. The thinking behind this is that this will give an additional amount of income to put aside to buy some form of annuity for the payee.

In Q -v- Q [2005] 2FLR640 a footballer who had been married for 10 years and had 4 children was ordered to pay 40% of his £1 million per annum income to his wife on an extendable 4-year term.

Why it is so difficult to add compensation into a maintenance calculation

In the case of W -v- W (Periodical payments; variation) [2010] 2FLR985 Moylan J dealing with an application by a wife for an upwards variation of an order for periodical payments which the husband opposed on the ground that his ex-wife was now earning what she would have done absence the marriage and motherhood rejected that argument saying that: -

"The question was whether ending the periodical payments was a fair outcome in all the circumstances in particular could the wife adjust to the loss without undue hardship".

He was not happy with the husband's argument that because the wife had reinstated her career, she no longer needed compensating for the period of time that she was not working. He indicated that the concept of relationship generated disadvantage wasn't intended to place a ceiling on a spouse or former spouses' claims by reference to what they would have been able to earn but to ensure that the court did not overlook the effect on a spouse of a lost career.

In the case of Hvorostovsky -v- Hvorostovsky [2009] 2FLR 1574 the wife who was a ballerina applied for an increase in periodical payments ordered in 2001 in the sum of £113,000.00 per annum. In 2001 Hvorostovsky the former world-famous opera singer had a gross income of £552,000.00 per annum. By the time of the application his income had increased to £1.36 million per annum. Mrs. Hvorostovsky was awarded an increase of maintenance to £120,000.00 per annum with £12,500.00 per annum for each child and a school fees order.

She had argued that she was entitled to a significant increase on the basis of compensation for having given up her career. On the facts the Courts of Appeal rejected her arguments but did state: -

"compensation for relationship related disadvantage may be a very important ingredient in many cases particularly in the assessment of the original division of capital and foreseeable income. If reflected at that stage, it will find its continuing reflection on a variation hearing without a fresh assessment."

Due to the fact the court rejected Mrs Hvorostovsky's arguments on compensation on this particular case the adjustment upwards was then based on the following facts: -

"The fundamental changes of circumstances that must be weighed in the judgment of a changes in the wife's budgeted needs and the changes in the husband's circumstances, here principally his hugely increased earnings and newly acquired second family. The exercise must be guided by the language of statute. A single factor of greater significance is the husband's greatly increased income".

Mr Justice Bodey commented: -

"there are of course cases where a concise analysis of the identified concept of "needs, contributions and sharing, is a necessary and helpful intellectual tool in written or verbal argument provided these concepts are not elevated to the status of heads of claim. However (because ancillary relief cases tend to be fact specific and depend essentially on the exercise of a broad discretion in the pursuit of fairness) there are also many cases where a lengthy over sophisticated approach of this type is an unnecessary diversion which burdens rather than assists the court".

The Court of Appeal reviewed Charles J's comments in Cornick -v- Cornick (3) [2001] 2FLR 1240; that just as an income fall justified an application for a downward variation so an income rise justified an upward variation and that in neither case was the outcome bounded by the family's standard of living immediately before the breakdown. The court should exercise its discretion in such cases by applying the words of the statute without using the concept of reasonable needs as a determinative or limiting factor.

The court rejected Mrs. Hvorostovsky's claim based on relationship related disadvantage and so her increase in the award only reflected her former husband's increased income although it was stated to be based on sharing principle.

In SA -v- PA (pre-marital agreement – compensation) 2014 EWHC392 Mostyn J considered a claim for compensation argued on behalf of the wife. She failed for the following reasons: -

"it will only be in a very rare and exceptional case when the principle will be capable of being successfully invoked.

Such a case will be one where the court can say without speculation i.e. with almost near certainty, that the claimant gave up a very high earning career which had it not been forgone would have led to earnings at least equivalent to that presently enjoyed by the Respondent.

Such a high earning career which have been practiced by the claimant over an appreciable period during the marriage. Proof of this track record is key. Once these findings have been made compensation will be reflected by fixing the periodical payment aware (or the multiplicand if this aspect is being capitalized by Duxbury), towards the top end of the discretionary bracket (applicable for a needs assessment on the facts of the case). Compensation ought not to be reflected by a premium or additional element on top of the needs-based award."

CHAPTER NINE
NEEDS ARE ELASTIC

Whilst the extraordinary case or Juffali -v- Juffali [2016] EW8C 1684 a decision of Roberts J may not seem to be relevant to the average practitioner in fact Lady Justice Roberts goes out of her way to explain how to apply Section 25. The relevant paragraphs are found at paragraph 66 to 79. This was a case where the husband's wealth was so large that the court was simply looking at how it was going to meet the concept of needs sharing and compensation and then create a clean break. In fact, Lady Justice Roberts decided only to deal with needs.

She summarised her understanding of Section 25 and emphasized as follows: -

"the first consideration in any assessment of needs must be the welfare of any minor child or children of the family."

After that the principle factors which are likely to impact on the court's assessment of needs are: -

(i) The length of the marriage;

(ii) The length of the period following the end of the marriage, during which the applicant spouse will be making contributions to the welfare of the family;

(iii)The standard of living during the marriage;

(iv) The age of the applicant;

(v) The available resources as defined by Section 25 (2) (a).

There is an inter relationship between the level at which future needs will be assessed and the period during which a court finds those needs will be met by the paying former spouse. The longer that period the more likely it is that a court will not assess those needs on the basis throughout of the standard of living which replicates that enjoyed during the currency of the marriage.

In this context it is entirely principled in terms of approach for the court to assess its award on the basis that needs, both in relation to housing and income, will reduce in future in an appropriate case".

Mrs Juffali wanted a clean break of £197 million, her claim was reduced to £53,330,000.00. Lady Justice Roberts emphasizing that she was assessing the child and the wife's needs in the context of the parties' marital standard of living and the husband's exceptionally large resources.

In the earlier case of L -v- L [2011] EWHC 2207 (FAM) a joint lives award for spousal maintenance was substituted with a lesser figure payable for 2 years and 5 months with a Section 28 1(A) bar by King J. The quantum was reduced on the basis that the trial judge had failed to properly assess the ability of the husband to make maintenance payments for life and had failed to consider Section 25 (A) or the explain why she had made a joint lives order.

Mrs Justice King held that a term maintenance order would give the wife the opportunity to make the family farm which had been run as a hobby produce an income for her and if she was unable to do so she would be able to sell the farm and rehouse herself and use the excess capital released to produce an income in another way. Her reasoning was also based upon the fact that the wife had worked and produced an income throughout the marriage.

In CR -v- SR [2013] EWHC 1155 (FAM) consideration was given to the fairness to both parties in quantifying periodical payments orders and in particularly the ability of the husband to pay.

Moylan J granted permission for the husband to appeal the District Judge's decision.

There had been a significant issue as to the real level of the husband's income, but on the basis that he could draw £5,700.00 per month leaving him with only £1,200.00 a month after the payment of his rent. It was noted by the Judge that the effect of the order was to provide the wife with all of the capital and also a significant imbalance in her favour with respect to the parties' income positions. In considering the needs of the parties he found that it is important to have regard to the needs of both parties. Furthermore, in circumstances where a court is making orders based upon estimates for future income (as is often the case where a husband's income is estimated by a forensic accountant) Moylan J was of the view that there needed to be a reasonable degree of caution exercised.

to make sure that the order which is made is (a) affordable and (b) does not result in an imbalance or an undue imbalance between the parties' respective future financial positions.

SS -v- NS [2014] EWHC 4183 (FAM).

In this case the wife was seeking half of the parties' capital, but she wanted that to include all of their liquid capital. The wife was also seeking maintenance of £60,000.00 per annum index linked for 27 years plus 40% of the husband's net bonus income going forwards. She did accept that the share of the bonus should be kept at £70,000.00 and that a sum equivalent to the cost of school fees should be deducted from her share of the bonus.

The husband's net income was £169,687.00 per annum plus he received bonuses. His counter proposal was the wife should have the following: -

(a) Maintenance of £24,000.00 per annum for 12 months.

(b) £18,000.00 per annum for the next 4 years.

(c) £12,000.00 per annum for the next 6 years.

At the end of that 11-year period he wanted there to be a clean break. In addition, he was prepared to give the wife 20% of any net cash bonus for a period of 3 years capped at £18,000.00.

The Judge awarded the following: -

- £30,000.00 per annum index linked to RPI for 11 years but with a right to the wife to extend the term.

- 20% of the husband's net bonus capped at £26,000.00 per annum for a period of 6 years on a clean break basis.

- £48,000.00 per annum for the children with the husband paying school fees as well.

Mostyn J divided the capital so that the wife had most of the liquid assets with sufficient being retained by the husband to pay a deposit on a house she ended up with approximately56% of the asset total.

The decision on capital was made to enable the wife to buy a house out-right and to provide the husband with a deposit. It was also calculated that the husband could raise a mortgage and pay it off in a relatively short period of time from his bonuses going forwards.

The Judge then went through where he believes the situation with respect to maintenance is at the current date. He does so by summarizing the history of why we have maintenance in this jurisdiction and gives his view as to the current way in which to apply the discretionary principles set out in Section 25 of the Matrimonial Causes Act 1973.

The relevant paragraph is paragraph 46 and the principles he sets out are as follows: -

"i) A spousal maintenance award is properly made where the evidence shows that choices made during the marriage have generated hard future needs on the part of the claimant. Here the duration of the marriage and the presence of children are pivotal factors.

ii) An award should only be made by reference to needs, save in a most exceptional case where it can be said that the sharing or compensation principle applies.

iii) Where the needs in question are not casually connected to the marriage, the award should generally be aimed at elevating significant hardship.

iv) In every case the court must consider a termination of spousal maintenance with a transition to independence as soon as it is just and reasonable. A term should be considered unless the payee would be unable to adjust without undue hardship to the ending of payments. A degree of (not undue) hardship in making the transition to independence is acceptable.

v) If the choice between an extendable term and a joint lives order is finally balanced the statutory steer should militate in favour of the former.

vi) The marital standard of living is relevant to the quantum of spousal maintenance, but it is not decisive. That standard should be carefully weighed against the desired object of eventual independence.

vii) The essential task of the judge is not merely to examine the individual items in the claimant's income budget but also to stand back and look at the global total and to ask if it represents a fair proportion of the respondent's available income which should got to the support of the claimant.

viii) Where the respondent's income comprises a base salary and a discretionary bonus the claimant's award maybe equivalently partitioned with needs as strict necessity being met from the base salary and additional, discretionary items being met from the bonus on a capped percentage basis.

ix) There is no criterion of exceptionality on an application to extend a term order. On such an application an examination should be made or whether the implicit premise of the original order and the ability of the payee to achieve independence had been impossible to achieve and, if so why.

x) On an application to discharge a joint life order an examination should be made of the original assumption that it was just too difficult to predict eventual independence.

xi) If the choice is between an extendable and a non-extendable term is finally balanced the decision should normally be in favour of the economically weaker party."

Within the same judgment Mostyn J is highly critical of percentage-based awards citing the problems that have arisen since the introduction of the Child Support Act 1991 to demonstrate how difficult it is to have a formulaic based system.

It can be seen from the blue print produced above that Mostyn J is trying his hardest to give clarity in this area of the law. It is however the case that he has indicated that the case of Fleming -v- Fleming decided by the Court of Appeal and subsequently endorsed by the House of Lords in the McFarlane case is something that practitioners do not need to be bound by. As already indicated in an earlier chapter it is far safer to consider that Fleming -v- Fleming is binding and find exceptional circumstances if possible, on applying to an extend a term order. It is also the case that he refers to (not undue) hardship. This clause is not in the statute and indeed has not been thought acceptable by the higher courts.

That said it is clearly the trend at the present time for the Family Division and lower courts to use this guidance and to consider that needs are elastic rather than looking at issues of sharing or compensation.

In the case of Wright -v- Wright [2015] EWCA CIV2001 a case that had wide press coverage. There were findings that although a life time order had been made (presumable to avoid the effect of the Fleming test) the District Judge that had ruled on the original order had made it clear that the wife was expected to work at some time in the future.

By the time of the husband's application to vary her maintenance downwards she had failed to do so. She was given a term order to end on the husband's retirement with her payments reducing on an annual basis until 2019 by Roberts J. The reported case is her application for leave to appeal which was refused. The case does not, contrary to how it was reported in the press, establish any new principles in particular with respect to the ending of joint lives maintenance orders. It is only Parliament that can bring such orders to an end.

It does however demonstrate the less generous approach since 2011 especially at Family Division level.

Another decision of Roberts J is AB -v- FC (short marriage; needs; stock piling) [2016] EWHC 3285. In this case she was dealing with the breakdown of a 19-month marriage where the husband was a professional footballer and there was a child of 22 months and there was insufficient capital to create the clean break. She ordered the husband to pay £164,000.00 per annum of which she advised the wife that she was to ear mark £80,000.00 for mortgage payments, with those "stock piling payments" to be protected for an 8 to 10-year period. She made the periodical payments on a joint lives basis and there was an order for £36,000.00 per annum for the child. In addition, she gave the wife the proceeds of sale of the family home, 36% of the proceeds of sale of the holiday home and £32,500.00 towards her costs.

In the case of Mills -v- Mills [2018] UKSC 38, the Supreme Court were looking at the wife's claim for a variation of her maintenance upwards following her use of her capital provision which by the time of her application was no longer in existence. Her lump sum of £230,000.00 having originally been provided to purchase her a mortgage free home. By the time of her application to vary upwards she was in rented accommodation and had a shortfall between her earnings, her maintenance and the amount she needed for rent.

The Court of Appeal had determined Mrs Mill's application on her neediness rather than looking into her foolish investments. They determine that her maintenance going forwards needed to be increased from £1,100.00 per month under the terms of the Court Order made in 2002 to £2,241.00 per month.

The husband was granted leave to appeal on the ground as whether the Court of Appeal should have allowed the wife's housing expenses given that the original order had provided her with sufficient to meet her housing needs by way of a capital order. At first instance the wife had failed in her application. The husband's appeal was allowed unanimously.

In the case of Mickovski -v- Lidell [2017] EWCA Civ 251, the wife was receiving £723.00 per month periodical payments of maintenance. When she started working full time the husband applied to end the maintenance payments however, he was unsuccessful because it was found that the wife had child care commitments and therefore, she continued to need the same level of maintenance despite the increase in her income because there remained a shortfall in her outgoings.

Waggott -v- Waggott [2018] EWCA CIB 727. In this decision of the Court of Appeal the lead judgment was made by Lord Justice Moylan and it gives a clear interpretation of McFarlane. In summary the wife was appealing a life time award of £175,000.00 per annum which had been ordered to meet her needs. Her claim was that she should be receiving £190,000.00 per annum plus 35% of her husband's bonus up to and including 2019 (payable in 2022). Her appeal failed and the husband's cross appeal against the life time order succeeded. The life time order was replaced with a term order which was to expire on the 1st March 2012 with a Section 28 1 (A) bar.

CHAPTER TEN
BONUSES AND HOW THEY AFFECT MAINTENANCE

The starting point with respect to how bonuses are treated in applications for financial settlement is the case of H-v-H (2007) 2FR548 this is a case where the wife was a homemaker who had given up her career as a teacher. The husband was a very successful banker. Charles J had to decide the way in which the future bonuses would be distributed and whether they would form part of the matrimonial pot. He determined that the wife should receive a run off share over 3 years post separation.

The Court of Appeal also considered these issues in the case of Waggott -v- Waggott. Lord Justice Moylan's lead decision as well as being a very helpful interpretation of the way in which compensation and sharing first introduced in the case of Miller-v-Miller; McFarlane-v-McFarlane [2006] 20C618 should be interpreted makes it clear that a bonus is not capable of being a matrimonial asset;

> "In my view there are a number of reasons why the clear answer is that it is not" (para 122)

He went on to state that: -

> "any extension of the sharing principle to post-separation earnings would fundamentally undermine the court's ability to effect a clean break" (para 123)

as he pointed out that this would in fact contradict Lady Hales observations in Miller that: -

> "It can be assumed that the marital partnership does not stay alive for the purpose of sharing future resources unless this is justified by need or compensation" (para 144) or Lady Hale's observation

as to the effect of "two strict an adherence to equal sharing" (para 142).

The Court of Appeal was dealing with Mrs Waggott's appeal against an order which provided her with a share of the capital resources in the sum of 8.4 million pounds and the husband received 7.8 million pounds. The wife also received a further 1.4 million pounds which was given to her by the trial judge as a share of the deferred remuneration owed to the husband after separation in 2012.

This gave her a total capital figure of 9.7 million pounds.

In addition to the capital figure the wife received life time maintenance in the sum of £175,000.00 per annum.

Her appeal was based on the fact that she believed that she should have received 35% of the husband's net bonus payable in respect of the years up to and including 2019 (to be received by the husband in 2022) plus an increase in her maintenance to £190,000.00 per year on a joint life's basis.

The husband cross appealed on the basis that his earning capacity (3.7 million pounds per annum in 2014) was not an asset to which the sharing principle applies albeit he did concede that as a matter of practice an award of post separation bonuses sometime occurs even though they were earnt during the marriage. Inter alia he was also arguing for a term maintenance order to be imposed with a Section 28 1(A) bar to come into effect in February 2021.

The trial judge had found that the wife could not adjust without undue hardship to the termination of maintenance given the life style she was accustomed to during the marriage.

The wife's argument for 35% of the husband's bonus up to 7 years post settlement rested on arguments of sharing and compensation. The trial judge had found sharing did not apply to post separation earnings and that any claim for maintenance in the case rested on needs.

The line of argument followed by the judge was that that had been put forwards by Mostyn J in the case of B-v-S [2012] EWHC26.

Although the trial judge in the Waggott case found that post separation earnings should be confined to providing for needs, he did allow for a share in the bonus received in 2014 and 2015 on the basis that assets should be the assets found to exist at the time of the hearing. His figures provided the wife with 25% of the bonus for 2014 and 12.5% for the bonus for 2015.

The Court of Appeal emphasized that although discrimination had been outlawed in White -v- White [2001] 1AC596605 this did not mean that judges do not have any ability to discriminate;

> "between different sets of facts and thus between different claims."

What is outlawed is discrimination on the ground of superficial differences which on analysis do not reflect substantive differences and that the "yardstick of equality" was to be applied to "unavailable assets" (paragraph 605).

The Court of Appeal also emphasized that Thorpe LJ had rejected the concept that the yardstick of equality could be applied to income in the McFarlane-v- McFarlane; Parlour -v- Parlour [2004] EWCA (civ) 872 decision. Albeit they recognized that a surplus of income over future needs could be made available to provide both parties with money to invest to achieve financial independence "within a relatively short span of time".

Arguments were considered from the husband's leading counsel with respect to the issue of the bonuses and emphasis was given to the question as to whether the sharing principle applied to bonuses earnt after separation.

In the case of Rossi -v- Rossi [2007] 1FL790 (paragraph 24.4) Mr Mostyn QC as he then was, acknowledged that there was an "element of arbitrariness" in dealing with bonuses however in that case he confirmed that he would not allow a post separation bonus to be classed as a matrimonial asset unless it related to a period which commenced less than 12 months after separation. He considered the 12 months period is too close to the marriage to justify it being treated as a non-matrimonial asset.

Note however that this was not followed by Charles J in H-v-H. In that case Mr. Justice Charles dealt with the bonuses by awarding the wife "declining percentages" from the husband's bonuses over a 3-year period. He justified this approach by reference to the concept of compensation and sharing (paragraph 111).

Bodey J in the case of CR-v-CR [2008] 1FRL323 emphasized the wife's reasonable requirements when considering the husband's high likely future earnings and he decided that the wife should have additional capital awarded on the basis of fairness and to reflect the husband's higher earnings.

The outcome of the wife's appeal in Waggott, as already explained, was that it failed.

The husband's cross appeal succeeded insofar as the wife's maintenance was turned into a term order until the end of February 2021 with a Section 28 1(A) bar. The Court of Appeal did not accept the trial judge's findings on undue hardship.

The wife did not get the 35% of the husband's bonus that she was seeking.

This case establishes that there is no automatic right to a share of bonuses that are earnt post separation on a sharing basis. This does not mean that they will not be taken into account where there is a need for maintenance which has been described as "elastic" by MostynJ in B-v-S and again in SS-v-NS [2014] EWHC4183 (FAM).

To recap in SS-v-NS the wife was seeking inter alia 40% of the husband's bonuses going forwards. She argued that this should be capped at £70,000.00 and she was prepared to concede that she would be responsible for paying the children's school fees from this sum. She wanted this share in addition to maintenance of £60,000.00 per annum. The husband was offering term maintenance for 11 years and 20% of his bonus for 3 years capped at £18,000.00.

The wife was awarded a term order of £30,000.00 per annum for 11 years with no Section 28 1(A) bar and 20% of the net bonus capped at £26,500.00 for 6 years with a clean break clause.

Mostyn J finding bonuses can be utilized to meet needs but;

> "where the respondent's income compromises a base salary and a discretionary bonus the claimant's award may be equivalently partitioned with needs of strict necessity being met from the base salary and additional discretionary items being met from the bonus on a capped percentage basis."

It is clear from reading Waggott-v-Waggott that there is no automatic right to a share of bonuses post separation albeit if they have been earnt prior to separation they do form part of the matrimonial assets Bonuses can be drawn on to meet needs of maintenance but on a term basis and the courts are more likely to make a Section 28 1(A) bar on that part of the maintenance that depends on a share of the bonus.

CHAPTER ELEVEN
COHABITATION

Periodical payments of maintenance are expressed to be during joint lives until the applicant remarries or further order.

As we have seen prior to the Matrimonial Causes Act 1973 maintenance orders were expressed as continuing "dum sola" or "casta vexerit".

Amongst many clients there is a strong belief that there should at least be a presumption that cohabitation is a change of circumstances that brings about a financial benefit to the payee with the consequence that not only is the level of maintenance reduced but that a joint lives order should be converted to a term order. Many people believe it is a matter or principle the payer should be released from their obligation to support their former spouse if he or she chooses to live with another person in a state that has all the appearance of a remarriage.

It is the case that cohabitation is not mentioned as a Section 25 factor and it is not referred to in Section 31, the provisions that deal with variation of maintenance. To advance an argument to justify variation on the basis of cohabitation it is necessary to do so by relying on the sweep up provisions which refer to all the circumstances of the case and "a change of circumstances".

Cohabitation was not dealt with by the amendments introduced in 1984.

The practitioner has to be aware that there are precedents available which enable the payer to offer to pay periodical payments which will end if the payee cohabits for a continuous period of x months. It is unwise to advise a client to accept such condition for a payee as it is unlikely that the court would impose one, particularly as once an order terminates it cannot be resurrected see CT -v- T 1988 1FLR 480.

In the case of MH -v- MH [1982] 3FLR 429 the wife was aged 46. She was cohabiting with a man aged 30 who had qualified as a chartered accountant but who had not been successful in his business. They were in a settled relationship for 4 years. A notional earning capacity was ascribed to the cohabitee and Wood J (as he then was) found that a fair just and reasonable approach could be applied by reducing the maintenance from £3,900.00 per annum to £500.00 per annum, however he left the joint lives order unaltered.

In Suter -v- Suter and Jones [1987] FAM111 [1987] 2All ER366 the wife was aged 31 with two children aged 14 and 18. She was cohabiting with a labourer from the Davenport dockyard. This arrangement was in place at the time that the original order was made. Following the 1984 amendment the Court of Appeal considered the fact that the wife had been provided with a lot of capital and that she was cohabiting and decided this justified a reduction in payment from £1,200.00 per annum to a nominal order. They found that it was reasonable to expect the cohabitee to make a reasonable financial contribution to the wife's household however they refused to reduce the length of the ten-year term order. The Court of Appeal held that if a wife cohabits with another man it is not necessarily a reason for reducing or terminating her maintenance as cohabitation is not to be equated with remarriage. They emphasized that there is not a statutory requirement that the court should give decisive weight to the fact of cohabitation and stated that if the court were to do so it would impose an unjustified fetter on the freedom of an ex wife to lead her own life how she chooses following a divorce. They indicated that an order which varied the order for periodical payments by reducing payments over a period of time would only be justified if in the opinion of the court the period during which the payments;

"would be sufficient to enable the party in whose favour the order was made to adjust without undue hardship to the termination of those payments".

Such an order should not be made if the wife had means of generating an income herself.

In the case of Atkinson -v- Atkinson (No 2) [1995] 2FLR356 the wife was aged 55. She was cohabiting with a 33-year-old man for 4 years after the ancillary relief hearing. She had no income. The original order had been for periodical payments of £30,000.00 for joint lives. At first instance on the husband's application this was reduced to £18,000.00 per annum on appeal a year later when there was more information obtained about the cohabitee's business Thorpe J further reduced the order to £10,000.00 per annum but he left the joint lives order unaltered stating: -

"in assessing the relevance of the cohabitation factor, it seems to me as much, if not more, weight must be given not to the presence of the cohabitee as to his financial circumstances, and his capacity to make reasonable contribution in return for the benefits to the provision of the home."

In Fleming and Fleming [2004] 1FLR 667 CA this case was principally about the wife's application to extend the term order where she had also been cohabiting for five years. Whilst her application failed Thorpe J emphasised in the course of his judgment as follows: -

"nor do I think that the decision of this court in Atkinson -v-Atkinson causes for visitation in the light of whatever social changes there may have been over the course of the last 15 years or so. The judgment of Waterhouse J on the point of principle is broadly expressed. His conclusion that cohabitation is not to be equated with marriage remains as sound today as it was then. Equally it seems to me that the direction of the court in assessing the impact of cohabitation should have with regard to the overall circumstances including financial consequences remains a proper course to be followed. Of course, in a case such as this where the length of cohabitation is greater than many a marriage that becomes before a court for assessment the range of discretion given to the judge available him or her to place considerable weight on that circumstance. There is no indication that His Honour Judge Michael Taylor did not regard the continuing cohabitation as is an essential feature of the case. The statutory distinction between remarriage which terminates financial obligation (by virtue of Section 28 of the Matrimonial Causes Act 1973) and cohabitation which does not, would fall for Parliamentary consideration if the Government's present plans to legislate rights and responses for same sex partners were extended to cohabitees".

To date there is no reported case where cohabitation per se has terminated the wife's joint lives maintenance order. It is not to be equated with marriage, it is relevant only insofar as it results in some diminution of the wife's needs either on account of financial support (actual or deemed reasonable) given by her cohabitee or because it was simply cheaper for people to live together as a joint household rather than to live separately.

The furore in the press about a decision of Mostyn J in AB -v- CB Trustees of re: ex trust [2014] EWHC 2998 (FAM) 2014 WL4636727 when the judge commented at paragraph 63 to 66 as the wife's possible intention to cohabit and describe the relationship she had with a third party as "a significant fly in the ointment in the assessment of need" was not in fact a decision about cohabitation in the light of a maintenance application.

In K -v- K [2006] 2FLR468 Coleridge J did consider the court's approach over the last 30 years was now outdated. He called for a reconsideration of the significance of cohabitation and for the first time in any reported judgment he considered that as a matter of principle cohabitation was a relevant factor on an application to vary or terminate a spousal maintenance order. Despite his comments concerning cohabitation what he did however was to reduce the periodical payments to £12,000.00 per year and capitalise those payments at the sum of £100,000.00. He did not do so on the Duxbury basis that would have given the wife £175,000.00. He indicated that the wife's cohabitation justified a reduction in the lump sum. Stating;

> "in the 35 years since the enactment a social revolution has taken place. The concept of cohabitation is now as normal common place and acceptable as marriage. At every level of society and amongst all adult age groups people cohabit without a second thought.
>
> It carries no social stigma whatever. In these circumstances should not the financial consequences of cohabitation (following the previous divorce) be the same as the financial consequence of a further marriage; namely that any then existing order be discharged or, one way or another, no longer remain effective?
>
> Finally, I will leave this part of the case by making these points:
>
> I see no reason why nowadays courts should not order a termination on "cohabitation" after a certain period. Section 28 of the Matrimonial Causes Act by no means prohibits it and it would at least provide certainty for the parties it would I consider it would better reflect modern laws and social behaviour. Much time has been spent on a consideration of the overall financial picture of the two households it seems to me in the modern climate that this is inevitable.
>
> It was the approach adopted in Fleming. If the court is to achieve fairness in these cases it must be in possession of the whole financial picture of both households. There is no longer any justification for shyness in the production of financial information where parties cohabit."

It is of course the case that box 4.6 of Form E requires those who have remarried and/or entered into a civil partnership or are living with another person or intend to do so to give "brief details so far as they are known to you or his or her income, assets and liabilities" this begs the question as to why if the courts are going to ignore cohabitation as these details are required. This has to be balanced with the case law and the relevance of the courts to invade the privacy of a new partner's financial affairs. See Frary -v- Frary [1993] 2FLR 696 and Wynne -v- Wynne and Jeffers [1990] 3 All E 659 and in fact despite the dicta that is quoted from above by Coleridge J the courts have continued to follow the earlier cases.

In the case of H -v- H [2009] EWHV 464 [2009] 2FLR 795 Singer J said that the relevance and effect of the wife's pregnancy by another man had to be viewed dispassionately. He was not prepared to find that the wife was cohabiting nor that her boyfriend was contributing to her living expenses he found that the pregnancy did not affect her income award. The husband was ordered to pay spousal maintenance of £125,000.00 per annum and child maintenance (for his children) of £15,000.00 per annum from a net income of £435,000.00 per annum. Singer J was not prepared to create a clean break as the wife would not be able to adjust without undue hardship to the termination of her financial dependents upon the husband.

The case went to the Court of Appeal as Gray -v- Gray [2009] EWCA CI1424 the appeal was successful in that the Court of Appeal said that the judge had asked himself the wrong question. The issue was not what the cohabitee was contributing to the wife's finances but what he should be contributing however they endorsed Singer J findings that it was for Parliament to change the law, despite the Court of Appeal having sympathy with Coleridge J views in K-v- K. The case was remitted to Singer J to consider the correct level of maintenance.

CHAPTER TWELVE
VARIATION OF PERIODICAL PAYMENTS

Applications for a variation of periodical payments are made under Section 31 of the Matrimonial Causes Act 1973. In previous chapters we have seen that the court has endorsed the case of Cornick -v- Cornick (No 3) which confirms that the court can take into an account an increase in wealth of the payer and that Section 25 (2) (c) namely the standard of living endured by the family before the breakdown of the marriage is by itself not a determining factor for example if the payer's available resources have decreased dramatically the payee would not be able to argue successfully against a downward variation because the payees standard of living would then fall below the standard endured by the family before the breakdown of the marriage. See Hvorostovskyi -v- Hvorostovsky.

It is therefore logical that the payee is not precluded from deriving benefit from an increase in the payer's fortunes even if this results in the payee enjoying a higher standard of living than she or he did during the marriage.

White -v- White is clear authority that on an application for a variation of a periodical payments order (and for an order for capitalization of periodical payments) for the following point namely that: -

The court should not rely on the judicial concept of "reasonable requirements" as a determinative or limiting factor in cases where a payer has or requires an ability to pay more than the paid financial needs even when they are interpreted generously and called "reasonable requirements" and the court should exercise its discretion by applying the words of the statute.

Many of the cases that we have already looked at in previous chapters are cases following a variation.

A variation is made on a form A1 with a Form E1 being completed following the directions of the court. Unfortunately, there is still a fee to pay of £255.00 and the process follows to a large extent the process of any application under Section 23 or Section 24. It can be an expensive way of obtaining an increase in maintenance indeed it can take an applicant many years before they have recouped the fees from the additional maintenance itself. Accordingly, alternative dispute resolution is a sensible way forward particularly mediation where such an application is contemplated.

As we have also seen in previous chapters there is no guarantee that an increase or an extension of maintenance where there is a term order will succeed indeed in the case of N -v N (financial orders: appellant role) [2011] EWCA CIV940 [2012] 1FR 622 the Court of Appeal heard a case where there had been a seven-year marriage. The consent order had included a recital that it was intended that the wife would become financially independent by working and that she would keep the husband informed as to any increase in her income over £1,000.00 net per month. On this basis he agreed to pay the wife £1,000.00 per calendar month for 5 years. No Section 28 (1) (A) bar was applied to the agreement. The wife applied to vary and extend her periodical payments before the end of the 5 years. At first instance the District Judge found that she had made no serious attempt to ensure that her skills were up to date or relevant and found that she was unwilling to work. He extended the 5-year term for just over a year but with a Section 28 (1) (A) bar. The Circuit Judge on appeal extended the term to 3 years and then imposed an order for nominal maintenance. In other words, he removed the Section 28 (1) (A) bar.

On appeal by the husband to the Court of Appeal his appeal was allowed as the circuit judge had failed to direct himself as to the nature of the appellate process and had based his decision on a view of the wife's financial situation that was fundamentally at variance with the findings of fact made by the district judge rather than finding that the district judge had misdirected herself on the legal issues.

Joy Morancho -v- Joy (dismissal of variation application) [2017] EWHC 2086 (FAM). This case is a warning to those who try to use an application to vary as a form of back door appeal.

In this case the husband had made an application to vary three months after the judgment in which he had been found to be profoundly dis-honest and found to have the ability to raise an income considerably more than that he had disclosed. The case had been heard by Sir Peter Singer who then heard the application for a variation. The case was case managed on the basis it would be an abbreviated procedure given the damning findings that had already been made against the husband. Sir Peter Singer clearly thought that the application was a disguised attempt to appeal, and he was reluctant to look at the case de novo on the basis that at the of the application the husband's circumstances had not changed although they had changed by the time of the hearing and this had to be taken into account. It was found that it was not sufficient to justify a variation. The case also reflects on the difficulty that a litigant will have on a variation application in getting around and adverse findings of fact about resources and credibility which have been made at the initial hearing.

The case of Morris -v- Morris [2016] EWCACIV 812 is another case determined by Moylan J (as he then was) where he found that there are applications for variation which can be dealt with by using a "light touch review" as opposed to considering the case de novo on the basis that the court must exercise proportionality.

CHAPTER THIRTEEN
CAPITALISATION

It is possible to apply to the court on a variation or indeed at the initial hearing for maintenance to be capitalised and a clean break to be affected. Indeed, it is the court's duty to try and achieve this result for the parties pursuant to section 25A MCA1973.

In the case of Pearce -v- Pearce [2004] 1WLR68 the Court of Appeal had to look at the wife's application for an increase in a capital settlement both by way of an additional lump sum and capitalized maintenance.

With respect to the application for the lump sum they made the following finding: -

> "there is simply no power or discretion to embark upon further adjustment of capital and reflect the outcome of unwise or unfortunate investment on one side or prudent and lucky investment on the other"

The wife had effectively dissipated all of her capital settlement.

With respect to the matter of her increase in maintenance however they stated that this could be dealt with by an application to vary upwards which could be capitalized with a lump sum order: -

> "Both as a matter of principle and as a matter of good practice, in my opinion the judge had to decide three questions in the following sequence. First, he had to decide what variation to make in the order for periodical payments agreed in 1997. An increase was inevitable given inflation and the husband's overall increased prosperity despite the decline in his income. The judges second task was to fix the date from which the increased order was to

commence. That would dispose of the past and present account between the parties. Then, and only then, should he have moved to the future, substituting a capital payment calculated in accordance with the Duxbury tables for the income stream he was terminating"

The lump sum that was awarded in lieu of maintenance amounted to £655,000.00.

As a matter of practice, it is important to advise clients who are making payments of maintenance following a final consent order or indeed a final decision of the judge to warn that client of the possibility of an application to vary and capitalise maintenance in the future. Whilst it is the case that a clean break of capital rights cannot be overturned, to a client a payment of £655,000.00 will seem as if he or she is making a further capital payment rather than capitalised maintenance.

In Cornick -v- Cornick (No 3) [2001] 2FLR1240 the wife applied to vary and capitalise her periodical payments order whilst the previous orders were relevant the court was not restricted by its findings as to their standard of living made in the course of the earlier proceedings and the court could take all relevant factors into account in reaching a fair decision relying on the decision of the House of Lords in the White case. The court took a caution approach with respect to the increase in payments used a broad calculation method with Duxbury the starting point to calculate the capital sum.

In W -v- W [2004] 1FLR494 the court increased the wife's periodical payments of £34,000.00 per annum and backdated the increase to the date of the application to vary capitalising payments at the sum of £564,00.000. The court stated in this case that it was necessary to look at the totality of the husband's resources in assessing his ability to pay and concluded that the husband had resources to continue to discharge the award.

In Lauder -v- Lauder [2007] 2FLR 802 the court assessed an income of about £60,000.00 per annum to be reasonable and capitalized maintenance at £725,000.00.

In the case of Vaughn-v- Vaughn [2010] EWCA CIV349 a couple had married in 1967 and they separated in 1981. The husband was paying maintenance of £27,000.00 per annum but succeeded at first instance in having the order discharged without a capital payment to the wife relying on his forthcoming retirement. The Court of Appeal allowed the wife's appeal and varied the order to £14,000.00 per annum and then capitalised it at £215,000.00 finding that the Deputy District Judge had made two errors. First of all, he should not have allocated half of the husband's pension to his second wife as priority cannot be given to a second wife who married in the knowledge of the claims of the first wife. Secondly it was wrong to amortize an inheritance received by the first wife. The husband argued that it should be amortized as the wife had no children. Lord Justice Wilson said it was "invidious for the court to try analysis a person's relationship in order to seek to measure the extend of reasonable expectations of benefit under her or his estate".

A helpful report where there is a modest income and capital to be shared between the parties is the case of A -v- L (departure from equality; needs) [2011] ELHC 315 O (FAM) 2012 AFLR in this case the court on appeal capitalised maintenance and terminated the periodical payments order by providing the wife with approximately 56% of the overall assets. This case demonstrates that the court is prepared to make a clean break on this basis in the more modest cases. The judge was Moore J he confirms in the course of the judgment that it was a difficult case because of the lack of assets and income. He also comments that he must "balance unfairness" between the parties.

It is the case that in recent years there is a stronger trend by the judiciary to look at the effect of maintenance orders not only on the payee but on the payer and that happened in this case.

In Yates -v- Yates [2012] EWCA CIV 532 the husband and wife had entered in to a consent order providing that the wife would receive a lump sum of £978,000.00 and a periodical payment order for a 3-year term. There was no bar on her applying for an extension of the term of the periodical payments order under Section 28 (1) (A).

It had been intended that the wife's lump sum would be used in part to discharge the mortgage on the former matrimonial home instead she chose to remortgage for £100,000.00 and she invested the balance of her lump sum in a non-income generating bond. She then applied to extend increase and capitalise her periodical payments of maintenance at first instance she was successful, and she was awarded a further lump sum of £450,000.00. That amount was reduced by the circuit judge on appeal, but he did not deduct the mortgage payments in calculating the lower lump sum. The husband appealed at the Court of Appeal contending that the District Judge has wrongly taken into account her continuing mortgage payments when calculating her budget. His appeal was successful, and the lump sum was further reduced.

The Court of Appeal had not heard an appeal against the wife's successful extension of the term to obtain her lump sum to 12 years and expressed concern about the same but could not deal with it.

Deliberate deflation of income to reduce an award of maintenance

Tattersall -v- Tattersall [2013] EWCA CIV 744.

In this case the parties were in their mid-30's and had been married for 10 years. They had one child who was 3½. They had disputed residence of their child but that was resolved by the time of the hearing. Both parties were employed. The wife worked at Oxford University she earnt £1,100.00 per calendar month after she had paid for nursery fees. She had a total net income which included child benefit and the husband's child support payments of £1,760.00 per calendar month. The husband earnt £2,400.00 per calendar month at the time of the hearing as a lecturer at Liverpool University however he had chosen not to do extra work that was available to him and had previously earned as much as £4,000.00 per calendar month for doing the same.

The parties had a substantial property portfolio however it was heavily geared and there was only £217,000.00 worth of equity therein. They did manage to agree about the division of their pension funds.

The circuit judge who heard the case decided that the wife would have to sell the properties in the portfolio to buy something suitable and her needs were assessed at £2,250.00 per month. An index linked periodical payments order was made in the sum of £1,070.00 per calendar month on an extendable term until the child reached 18. The judge also divided the capital as to 30% to the husband and 70% to the wife on the basis of needs. She found that the husband could have a higher income and earning capacity and she refused to make a Mesher Order in his favour.

The husband appealed and his appeal was based on the fact that he was being asked to pay too much maintenance for too long and that there should have been a Mesher Order. He argued that the wife's child care costs would decrease when the child started school. Black LJ gave the lead judgment the appeal was dismissed partially because the husband had sought to advance arguments that had not been before the circuit judge it is clear that they felt the order was generous but within the judge's discretion. This is a useful case where you have a payer who deliberately deflates their income.

Reclaiming Overpayments

In the case of G -v- P [2013] EWCC HHJ Barnett the husband successfully used Section 33 and Section 38 of the Matrimonial Causes Act 1973 to justify an order where the maintenance had been overpaid for a year after the wife had remarried to obtain the repayment thereof. Given this decision it may be worth in some circumstances considering an application for repayment where there is a successful variation down-wards.

It is also worth remembering the concern express by Charles J in MT -v- T where the wife's claim for financial provision was dismissed at final hearing at the foreign marriage was held to not to constitute a marriage at all. During the proceedings the husband had paid her more than £900,000.00 in MPS and legal services payments. Charles J indicated that in special circumstances the Court of Appeal's decision that interim maintenance payments were recoverable could be over-ridden particularly when the payments were for costs.

CHAPTER FOURTEEN
THE TREATMENT OF BONUSES
IN FINANCIAL SETTLEMENT

The starting point with respect to how bonuses are treated in applications for financial settlement is the case of H-v-H (2007) 2FR548 this is a case where the wife was a homemaker who had given up her career as a teacher. The husband was a very successful banker. Mr Justice Charles had to decide the way in which the future bonuses would be distributed and whether they would form part of the matrimonial pot. He determined that the wife should receive a run off share over 3 years post separation.

The Court of Appeal has recently considered these issues in the case of Waggott and Waggott [2018] EWCACIV727. Lord Justice Moylan has provided the lead decision. It is a very helpful interpretation of the way in which compensation and sharing first introduced in the case of Miller-v-Miller; McFarlane-v-McFarlane [2006] 20C618 should be interpreted.

The Court of Appeal decided in Waggott contrary to arguments put forward on behalf of the wife's leading counsel that the husband's future earnings were not capable of being a matrimonial asset;

> "In my view there are a number of reasons why the clear answer is that it is not"

per Lord Justice Moylan (para 122)

Lord Justice Moylan went on to state that: -

> "any extension of the sharing principle to post-separation earnings would fundamentally undermine the court's ability to effect a clean break" (para 123)

as he pointed out that this would in fact contradict Lady Hales observations in Miller that: -

> "It can be assumed that the marital partnership does not stay alive for the purpose of sharing future resources unless this is justified by need or compensation" (para 144) or Lady Hale's observation as to the effect of "two strict an adherence to equal sharing" (para 142).

In the Waggott case the Court of Appeal was dealing with the wife's appeal against an order which provided her with a share of the capital resources in the sum of 8.4 million pounds and the husband received 7.8 million pounds. The wife also received a further 1.4 million pounds which was given to her by the trial judge as a share of the deferred remuneration owed to the husband after separation in 2012.

This gave her a total capital figure of 9.7 million pounds.

In addition to the capital figure the wife received life time maintenance in the sum of £175,000.00 per annum.

Her appeal was based on the fact that she believed that she should have received 35% of the husband's net bonus payable in respect of the years up to and including 2019 (to be received by the husband in 2022) plus an increase in her maintenance to £190,000.00 per year on a joint lives' basis.

The husband cross appealed on the basis that his earning capacity (3.7 million pounds per annum in 2014) was not an asset to which the sharing principle applies albeit he did concede that as a matter of practice an award of post separation bonuses sometime occurs even though they were not earnt during the marriage. Inter alia he was also arguing for a term maintenance order to be imposed with a Section 28 1(a) bar to come into effect in February 2021.

The trial judge had found that the wife could not adjust without undue hardship to the termination of maintenance given the life style she was accustomed to during the marriage.

The wife's argument for 35% of the husband's bonus up to 7 years post settlement rested on arguments of sharing and compensation. The trial judge had found sharing did not apply to post separation earnings and that any claim for maintenance in the case rested on needs.

The line of argument followed by the judge was that put forwards a Mr Justice Mostyn in the case of B-S [2012] EWHC265 when he stated that: -

> "the reason that the sharing principle is sometimes advocated as being applicable to a periodical payments claim is to reflect the theory that post-separation earnings derive from an earning capacity built up during the marriage which is in some intangible way a piece of matrimonial property there to be equitably or fairly shared. The high point of that theory is the dictum of Lady Hale (*in McFarlane*). As a theory it is problematic because at the end of the day the only reason there is income after separation is because of work done after separation. A footballer who earns £100,000.00 per annum earns that because he is on the pitch. Certainly, the skills he was born with and the development of those skills (which may have happened during his marriage) are all reasons why he can command his salary, but he will not get paid it unless he plays football. The footballer has to fill the unforgiving minute with 60 seconds worth of distance run after the marriage".

Although the trial judge in the Waggott case found that post separation earnings should be confined to providing for needs, he did allow for a share in the bonus received in 2014 and 2015 on the basis that assets should be the assets found to exist at the time of the hearing. His figures provided the wife with 25% of the bonus for 2014 and 12.5% for the bonus for 2015.

The Court of Appeal emphasised that although discrimination had been outlawed in White -v- White [2001] 1AC596605 this did not mean that judges do not have any ability to discriminate "between different sets of facts and thus between different claims." What is outlawed is discrimination on the ground of superficial differences which on analysis do not reflect substantive differences and that the "yardstick of equality" was to be applied to "unavailable assets" (paragraph 605).

The Court of Appeal also emphasised that Thorpe LJ had rejected the concept that the yardstick of equality could be applied to income in the 2005 McFarlane-v- McFarlane; Parlour -v- Parlour decision. Albeit he recognized that a surplus of income over future needs could be made available to provide both parties with money to invest to achieve financial independence "within a relatively short span of time".

Arguments were considered from the husband's leading counsel with respect to the issue of the bonuses and emphasis was given to the question as to whether the sharing principle applied to bonuses earnt after separation.

In the case of Rossi -v- Rossi [2007] 1FL790 (paragraph 24.4) Mr Mostyn QC as he then was, acknowledged that there was an "element of arbitrariness" in dealing with bonuses however in that case he confirmed that he would not allow a post separation bonus to be classed a matrimonial asset unless it related to a period which commenced less than 12 months after separation. He considered the 12 months period is too close to the marriage to justify it being treated as a non-matrimonial asset.

Note however that this was not followed by Mr Justice Charles in H-v-H in that case Mr Justice Charles helped with the bonuses by awarding the wife "declining percentages" from the husband's bonuses over a 3-year period. He justified this approach by reference to the concept of compensation and sharing (paragraph 111).

Mr Justice Bodie in the case of CR-v-CR [2008] 1FRL323 emphasised the wife's reasonable requirements when considering the husband's high likely future earnings and he decided that the wife should have additional capital awarded on the basis of fairness and to reflect the husband's higher earnings.

The final outcome of the wife's appeal in Waggott was that it failed. The husband's cross appeal succeeded insofar as the wife's maintenance was turned into a term order until the end of February 2021 with a Section 21 1(a) bar awarded. The Court of Appeal did not accept the trial judge findings on undue hardship.

The wife did not get the 35% of the husband's bonus that she was seeking.

This case clearly confirms that there is no automatic right to a share of bonuses that are earnt post separation on a sharing basis.

This does not mean that they will not be taken into account where there is a need for maintenance which has been described as "elastic" by Mr Justice Mostyn in B-v-S and again in SS-v-NS [2014] EWHC4183 (FAM).

In SS-v-NS the wife was seeking inter alia 40% of the husband's bonuses going forwards. She argued that this should be capped at £70,000.00 and she was prepared to concede that she would be responsible for paying the children's school fees from this sum. She wanted this share in addition to maintenance of £60,000.00 per annum.

The husband was offering term maintenance for 11 years and 20% of his bonus for 3 years capped at £18,000.00.

The wife was awarded a term order of £30,000.00 per annum for 11 years but with no Section 28 1(a) bar and 20% of the net bonus capped at £26,500.00 for 6 years with a clean break clause.

The case provides a detailed history of maintenance in this jurisdiction and at paragraph 46 gives a careful analysis of the current law. There is emphasis in this paragraph that sharing, and compensation are rarely relevant.

With respect to bonuses these are to meet needs and;

> "where the respondent's income compromises a base salary and a discretionary bonus the claimant's award may be equivalently partitioned with needs as strict necessity being met from the base salary and additional discretionary items being met from the bonus on a capped percentage basis."

It is clear from reading Waggott-v-Waggott that there is no automatic right to a share of bonuses post separation albeit if they have been earnt prior to separation they do form part of the matrimonial assets.

Bonuses can be utilised to meet needs of maintenance but on a term basis and the courts are more likely to make a Section 28 1(a) bar on that part of the maintenance that depends on a share of the bonus.

CHAPTER FIFTEEN
PENSIONS

Don't forget that the main point of a pension is to provide income in retirement.

Occupational pensions divide into two main types defined benefits schemes where the pension is calculated to the fraction of the employer's final salary and money purchase schemes whether an individual pension fund is used to provide a pension.

Personal pensions always operate on a money purchase basis.

It is almost always worth getting an expert's advice not only on CEV values but providing a detailed breakdown of income forecast.

Remember in the case of a defined benefit scheme the amount that can be taken as a tax-free lump sum varies from scheme to scheme and is based on service. Thereafter the pension scheme member will have to take his or her pension as the pension is usually paid monthly. In such scheme's pensions are usually index linked. The pension schemes in the public services for example local government, the civil service, armed forces, police, the fire service, teaching profession and NHS are all "defined benefit schemes".

The money that is going to be received from such a pension is more relevant than its CEV. You will need an expert to advise you.

Money purchase schemes include both occupational and private pensions and each member has a fund from which the pension is paid. There are two ways in which such a pension can be taken: -

1. Through the purchase of an annuity in this case the pension scheme member uses the pension fund to buy annuity to

provide him or her with an income for the rest of their life. This income can be at a flat rate or increase with inflation.

2. It can be used to provide a widow, widowers or surviving civil partners pension. These choices affect the level of the pension since index linking will lead to a lower level of pension at the start and a flat rate pension and providing for an additional life e.g. widow (widower) or surviving civil partner it could also lead to a reduction in the amount of the regular pension payment.

Since April 2012 the drawdown rules have changed, and the amount is now limited to 100% of the Government Actuary department (GAD) rate. This means that people who have been in drawn down for the last few years are likely to see a large fall in income at their next review.

From April 2012 those over 55 have been able to draw capital of over 25% albeit there will be tax to pay at the highest rate. Practitioners need to be vigilant that pension funds do not disappear offshore during proceedings.

The Basic State Pension

This is a contributed pension which people earn through the payment of National Insurance contributions or being entitled to credits for these. To find out what the parties are entitled to a Form BR19 should be completed. This is available on line from the DWP on www.thepensionservice.gov.uk/resourcescentre/br19/home.asp

The basic state pension cannot be shared but you need to take it into account when working out your client's future income. You may need some expert advice.

<u>Pensions as income</u>

All pension income is taxable as income at your highest marginal rate.

A lump sum drawn down of over 25% of the fund will be taxed at the highest marginal rate.

When acting for an older couple the pre-occupation will be at the level of income that would be payable in retirement and consequently the main enquiry will often be what percentage of a pension the pension order will provide to provide equality of income in retirement. Client's need to know what the income will likely be. Again, clients need the assistance of an IFA or an actuary to calculate these figures. If there is to be a substantial Pension Sharing Order and ongoing spousal maintenance you need to ask if that spousal maintenance should be a joint lives order or should it be a term order to expire when the beneficiary of the Pension Sharing Order can take his or her pension or at the age when it will be appropriate for him to take a pension.

Such an order could be an extendable term order.

There is no case law on this point.

A Pension Sharing Order will normally mean that the beneficiary has to put her pension credit into a personal pension since most occupational pensions do not permit internal transfers.

If she does so as the law stands at present, she can take pension benefits from age 55. She could also take the tax-free lump sum from the same age that is 55. Doing either or both of these things will diminish the value of the pension income she will receive at retirement. This may then rebound on the paying spouse who will be expected to pay more after retirement age than would otherwise be the case. Again, expert advice will be needed.

If it is intended that a Pension Sharing Order is to provide income in retirement and not to provide a tax-free lump sum or income before retirement, then this needs to be clear and pointed out. If the order is agreed it can be recorded in a pre-amble to the order. If the order is not agreed it should be stated clearly to the judge at trial so that he or she can take this into account and hopefully express a view.

Remember Pension Sharing Orders cannot be deferred so this is a matter that has to be determined at the time of the order albeit it is possible to deal with the application for a pension share at a later date.

Where there are younger couples the issue as to provision as maintenance is unlikely to be the issue. You are instead looking at a pension more from the point of view of set off and capital.

CHAPTER SIXTEEN
BANKRUPTCY

A bankrupt's property does not include the ability to pursue an application for a financial remedy in divorce. D (JH)-v- D (S) [1973] 1 All ER 349 established that applications for financial relief are essentially personal in nature arising between the parties of the marriage. The bankrupt can issue proceedings for periodical payments of maintenance.

Applications for Maintenance Pending Suit and Periodical payments for bankruptcy purposes are defined as family proceedings by Section 281 (8) of the Insolvency Act 1986. As such they are none provable debts in the bankruptcy.

In the case of Albert -v- Albert [1997] 2 FLR 791 the Trustee in Bankruptcy tried to stay a wife's application for periodical payments of maintenance and sought to be joined into the proceedings. On appeal it was found that because the Trustee in Bankruptcy had not made an application for an income payments order in the bankruptcy and the wife was not making any application against the bankrupt's capital and as there were no issues to be determined between the Trustee and the Bankrupt or his wife it was a misconception on the part of the Trustee in Bankruptcy to intervene. It was for the Family Division to decide on the proportion of income to go to the wife. The amount of income available would be determined by any order the bankruptcy court had made by way of an Income Payments Order.

Although arrears of periodical payments are not provable in the bankruptcy and therefore theoretically can be enforced against the bankrupt after discharge leave will be needed to enforce arrears of maintenance that are more than 1-year old. Section 32 (1) Matrimonial Causes Act 1973.

The court maybe persuaded that the bankruptcy was a special circum-stance to warrant the granting of leave, but it will also be necessary to persuade the court that the debtor was in a position to pay. Charilaou -v Charilaou [2000] WL 1212893.

It is the case that although periodical payments are not provable debts against the bankrupt estate bankruptcy usually leads to an existing order being varied or stayed by the bankruptcy court.

CHAPTER SEVENTEEN
THE CHILD SUPPORT ACT 1991

All applications for maintenance for a large category of children come under the Child Maintenance Service ("CMS") which was created in 2008. It is part of the Department for Work and Pensions("DWP"). The relevant statute being the Child Support Act 1991.

The CMS is responsible for all new applications which have commenced since the 25th November 2013. It is for that reason that the history of the Child Support Agency is not relevant for this chapter as it no longer has jurisdiction.

The formula applied by the CMS in calculating maintenance for children is based upon a paying parent's gross weekly income less pension contributions for those earning more than £200.00 per week is.

- 12% for one qualifying child

- 16% for two qualifying children.

- 19% for three or more qualifying

for earnings up to £800.00 per week.

If earnings exceed £800.00 per week there is a two-stage calculation the same percentage formula is applied to the first £800.00 and the income in excess of £800.00 has the following percentage applied.

- 9% for one qualifying child

- 12% for two qualifying children

- 15% for three or more qualifying children

If there are other children supported by the paying parent

The paying parent must be receiving child benefit for the child or children living with them. The paying parent must be earning £200.00 - £3,000.00 gross per week. The paying parent would then receive an allowance for that child or children as follows: -

- 11% for one child

- 14% for two children

- 16% for three or more children

The allowance is deducted from the gross figure before the calculation is carried out, income over £156,000.00 gross per annum (£3,000.00) per week is exempt from calculation.

There is a reduction on the percentage calculation if income is between £100.00 and £199.99 gross per week a flat rate of £7.00 per week if income is between £7.00 and £100.00 gross per week.

There is no payment to make if income is below £7.00.

Shared Care Allowance

There is a shared care allowance given to the paying parent where the child or children stay at least one night per week with them. The allowance is calculated as follows: -

- 52 to 103 nights per annum 1/7th deduction

- 104 to 155 nights per annum 2/7th deduction

- 156 to 174 nights per annum 3/7th deduction

Where the child or children stay for 175 nights or more the deduction is 50% plus an extra £7.00 per week deduction for each child. If the paying parent is paying on the flat rate, then no maintenance will be due.

If the parents cannot agree on how many nights per annum the child or children are staying with the paying parent there will be an assumed share care assessment done allowing a deduction of only 1/7th. In these circumstances it is for the paying parent to produce either written evidence or a court order regarding the amount of shared care.

The CMS has been granted the power to obtain income information about the paying parent from HMRC to establish gross earnings and it is doing so.

If the paying parent wishes to challenge the figure obtained from HMRC there must be a difference of 25% less or more gross income actually recovered by the paying parent.

When does the CMS have jurisdiction

The CMS has jurisdiction to do a maintenance calculation where there is a qualifying child. Where the CMS has jurisdiction the jurisdiction of the court is limited by Section 8 of the Child Support 1991 ("CSA 1991").

A qualifying child is one who lives with only one or neither of his natural or adopted parents, CSA 1991 Section 3 and must be under 16, CSA 1991 Section 55 (1) or under 20 and receiving full time secondary education CSA Section 55 (1) and living in the jurisdiction apart form the paying parent who must also live in the jurisdiction.

A paying parent is classed as being in the jurisdiction if he or she is employed in the Civil Diplomatic or Armed Services to the Crown or is employed by a company registered in the UK CSA Section 44 (2) (A).

When looking at maintenance one has to be able to advise the court on Form E as to the CMS liability. Therefore, it is important that the court has an idea of the income that will come in from the paying parent to the parent with care.

It is important to remember that the CMS cannot take jurisdiction for:-

- Stepchildren

- Married children

- Children living outside the jurisdiction

- Children of a deceased paying parent

- Children of a paying parent outside the jurisdiction

- Disabled children who are not in education and who are over the age of 16 or who are over 20

- Children in tertiary education who are aged 16 to 20

- Children where there is an order which pre-dates 3rd March 2003

- Children where there is an order that post dates the 3rd March 2003 which is less than 12 months old.

Maintenance for all these children can be obtained by agreement or alternatively by application to the court. Applications can be made to the court if:

- The parties have agreed a maintenance figure and want that agreement to be made into a court order under CSA Section 8 (5)

- The CMS has jurisdiction and the paying parent's gross income exceeds £156,000.00 per annum. CSA Section 8 (6)

- The child has expenses that have that arise in vocational training even if they are in gainful employment.

- The paying parent is deceased.

- The child is in tertiary education.

- The child is disabled and over 16 and not in education or over 20 and dependent on the person making the application.

Also note Dickson -v- Rennie [2014] EWHC 4306 (Fam) where Holman J found that the court could not deal with top up maintenance until an assessment was done by the CMS. The meaning of this is that if you want to apply for top up maintenance because the paying parent is receiving a gross income of more than £3,000.00 per week then you will need to get the assessment done before you make your application.

Another important rule that you need to understand is that before March 2003 agreements registered as court orders kept client's out of the administrative scheme of the CSA. As a result, very few family practitioners developed a knowledge of the regulations or the workings of the CSA especially as it had developed such a bad reputation for failing to collect payments or to make assessments, and for inaccuracies when calculations were made.

In March 2003 the Child Support and Pensions Security Act 2000 ("the2000 Act") introduced CSA 1991 Section 4 (10) (aa). Since the 1st March 2003 it has been possible for either parent to apply for an assessment after the court order has been in force for more than 12 months.

Since this date it has become imperative for family practitioners to understand how the administrative law surrounding child support can affect negotiated settlements and can provide a door to negligence claims.

It is vitally important that clients have full information given to them regarding this power. Practitioners need to fully understand when advising clients regarding financial settlement in particular maintenance, that those with children know what to do about obtaining financial support from the paying parent for a child or children.

The first port of call is to go to CM options. This has a dedicated telephone helpline 0800 9880988 – and a website www.cmoptions.org to which the applicant can be referred.

There are a wide range of options provided on the website primarily engaged in encouraging the benefit of a private arrangement agreement. There is a form available on the website for such an agreement and there are links to other organizations. Your client will need to provide you with one of these assessments in order to complete your Form E.

One of the objectives of the CMS is to encourage and support the making and keeping by parents of appropriate voluntary maintenance arrangements. This is backed with flexibility given to the CMS to write off arrears and to accept part payment of arrears to encourage voluntary agreements.

Family bases agreements can be converted into court orders although this is not promoted by CM options or the CMS.

If agreements cannot be reached, then the client needs to apply to the CMS to do an assessment.

The whole system is set up so that clients can make these applications themselves.

There is no need for the solicitor to assist at this stage.

If the client is unhappy with the assessment, then the CMS will guide them through the appeal system. You need to advise your client to work within the time frames given by the CMS as these are short and an appeal after 12 months is impossible.

If you are acting for the paying parent, you must advise the paying parent that they must keep in touch with the CMS as it is a criminal offence not to advise as to a change of address and indeed changes in employment and increases in wages. Furthermore, the CMS do not have to prove actual service of an application upon the paying parent if service is made at the paying parents last known or notified address.

It is also important that you advise a paying parent of the draconian powers of enforcement now held by the CMS.

In certain circumstances a paying parent might want to allow the CMS to do a default maintenance decision as such decisions provide £39.00 per week for one child, £49.00 for two children or £51.00 for three or more qualifying children.

The receiving parent does have some rights with respect to dealing with a default maintenance payment and so does the court who can consider on looking at financial contributions made by the paying parent as to the level of maintenance needed for the paying parent.

Whilst it is not possible for the court to override the Child Support Act following the removal of its jurisdiction there is always the possibility of seeking a global maintenance order. That is an order that determines the amount of money that is needed by the family as a whole the court then makes an order that the spousal maintenance will go up or down in accordance with the CMS assessment. This is particularly helpful where a paying parent has deliberately had default maintenance payment made to reduce their real liability.

MORE BOOKS BY
LAW BRIEF PUBLISHING

A selection of our other titles available now:-

'A Practical Guide to the SRA Principles, Individual and Law Firm Codes of Conduct 2019 – What Every Law Firm Needs to Know' by Paul Bennett
'A Practical Guide to Licensing Law for Commercial Property Lawyers' by Niall McCann & Richard Williams
'A Practical Guide to Adoption for Family Lawyers' by Graham Pegg
'Essential Motor Finance Law for the Busy Practitioner' by Richard Humphreys
'A Practical Guide to Industrial Disease Claims' by Andrew Mckie & Ian Skeate
'Employment Law and the Gig Economy' by Nigel Mackay & Annie Powell
'A Practical Guide to the Law of Armed Conflict' by Jo Morris & Libby Anderson
'A Practical Guide to Redundancy' by Philip Hyland
'A Practical Guide to Vicarious Liability' by Mariel Irvine
'A Practical Guide to Claims Arising from Delays in Diagnosing Cancer' by Bella Webb
'A Practical Guide to Applications for Landlord's Consent and Variation of Leases' by Mark Shelton
'A Practical Guide to Relief from Sanctions Post-Mitchell and Denton' by Peter Causton
'Butler's Equine Tax Planning: 2nd Edition' by Julie Butler
'A Practical Guide to Equity Release for Advisors' by Paul Sams
'A Practical Guide to Immigration Law and Tier 1 Entrepreneur Applications' by Sarah Pinder
'A Practical Guide to Unlawful Eviction and Harassment' by Stephanie Lovegrove
'In My Backyard! A Practical Guide to Neighbourhood Plans' by Dr Sue Chadwick
'A Practical Guide to the Law Relating to Food' by Ian Thomas

'A Practical Guide to the Ending of Assured Shorthold Tenancies'
by Elizabeth Dwomoh

'Commercial Mediation – A Practical Guide' by Nick Carr

'A Practical Guide to Financial Services Claims' by Chris Hegarty

'The Law of Houses in Multiple Occupation: A Practical Guide to HMO
Proceedings' by Julian Hunt

'A Practical Guide to Unlawful Eviction and Harassment' by Stephanie Lovegrove

'A Practical Guide to Solicitor and Client Costs' by Robin Dunne

'Artificial Intelligence – The Practical Legal Issues' by John Buyers

'A Practical Guide to Wrongful Conception, Wrongful Birth and Wrongful Life
Claims' by Rebecca Greenstreet

'Occupiers, Highways and Defective Premises Claims: A Practical Guide Post-
Jackson – 2nd Edition' by Andrew Mckie

'A Practical Guide to Financial Ombudsman Service Claims'
by Adam Temple & Robert Scrivenor

'A Practical Guide to the Law of Enfranchisement and Lease Extension'
by Paul Sams

'A Practical Guide to Marketing for Lawyers – 2nd Edition'
by Catherine Bailey & Jennet Ingram

'A Practical Guide to Advising Schools on Employment Law' by Jonathan Holden

'Certificates of Lawful Use and Development: A Guide to Making and
Determining Applications' by Bob Mc Geady & Meyric Lewis

'A Practical Guide to the Law of Dilapidations' by Mark Shelton

'A Practical Guide to the 2018 Jackson Personal Injury and Costs Reforms'
by Andrew Mckie

'A Guide to Consent in Clinical Negligence Post-Montgomery'
by Lauren Sutherland QC

'A Practical Guide to Running Housing Disrepair and Cavity Wall Claims:
2nd Edition' by Andrew Mckie & Ian Skeate

'A Practical Guide to the General Data Protection Regulation (GDPR)'
by Keith Markham

'A Practical Guide to Digital and Social Media Law for Lawyers' by Sherree Westell

'A Practical Guide to Holiday Sickness Claims – 2nd Edition'
by Andrew Mckie & Ian Skeate

'A Practical Guide to Inheritance Act Claims by Adult Children Post-Ilott v Blue Cross' by Sheila Hamilton Macdonald

'A Practical Guide to Elderly Law' by Justin Patten

'Arguments and Tactics for Personal Injury and Clinical Negligence Claims'
by Dorian Williams

'A Practical Guide to QOCS and Fundamental Dishonesty' by James Bentley

'A Practical Guide to Drone Law' by Rufus Ballaster, Andrew Firman, Eleanor Clot

'Practical Mediation: A Guide for Mediators, Advocates, Advisers, Lawyers, and Students in Civil, Commercial, Business, Property, Workplace, and Employment Cases' by Jonathan Dingle with John Sephton

'Practical Horse Law: A Guide for Owners and Riders' by Brenda Gilligan

'A Comparative Guide to Standard Form Construction and Engineering Contracts'
by Jon Close

'A Practical Guide to Compliance for Personal Injury Firms Working With Claims Management Companies' by Paul Bennett

'A Practical Guide to the Landlord and Tenant Act 1954: Commercial Tenancies'
by Richard Hayes & David Sawtell

'A Practical Guide to Personal Injury Claims Involving Animals' by Jonathan Hand

'A Practical Guide to Psychiatric Claims in Personal Injury' by Liam Ryan

'Introduction to the Law of Community Care in England and Wales'
by Alan Robinson

'A Practical Guide to Dog Law for Owners and Others' by Andrea Pitt

'Ellis and Kevan on Credit Hire – 5th Edition' by Aidan Ellis & Tim Kevan

'RTA Allegations of Fraud in a Post-Jackson Era: The Handbook – 2nd Edition'
by Andrew Mckie

'RTA Personal Injury Claims: A Practical Guide Post-Jackson' by Andrew Mckie

'On Experts: CPR35 for Lawyers and Experts' by David Boyle

'An Introduction to Personal Injury Law' by David Boyle

'A Practical Guide to Claims Arising From Accidents Abroad and Travel Claims'
by Andrew Mckie & Ian Skeate

'A Practical Guide to Cosmetic Surgery Claims' by Dr Victoria Handley
'A Practical Guide to Chronic Pain Claims' by Pankaj Madan
'A Practical Guide to Claims Arising from Fatal Accidents' by James Patience
'A Practical Approach to Clinical Negligence Post-Jackson' by Geoffrey Simpson-Scott
'A Practical Guide to Personal Injury Trusts' by Alan Robinson
'Employers' Liability Claims: A Practical Guide Post-Jackson' by Andrew Mckie
'A Practical Guide to Subtle Brain Injury Claims' by Pankaj Madan
'The Law of Driverless Cars: An Introduction' by Alex Glassbrook
'A Practical Guide to Costs in Personal Injury Cases' by Matthew Hoe
'A Practical Guide to Alternative Dispute Resolution in Personal Injury Claims – Getting the Most Out of ADR Post-Jackson' by Peter Causton, Nichola Evans, James Arrowsmith
'A Practical Guide to Personal Injuries in Sport' by Adam Walker & Patricia Leonard
'The No Nonsense Solicitors' Practice: A Guide To Running Your Firm' by Bettina Brueggemann
'Baby Steps: A Guide to Maternity Leave and Maternity Pay' by Leah Waller
'The Queen's Counsel Lawyer's Omnibus: 20 Years of Cartoons from The Times 1993-2013' by Alex Steuart Williams

These books and more are available to order online direct from the publisher at www.lawbriefpublishing.com, where you can also read free sample chapters. For any queries, contact us on 0844 587 2383 or mail@lawbriefpublishing.com.

Our books are also usually in stock at www.amazon.co.uk with free next day delivery for Prime members, and at good legal bookshops such as Wildy & Sons.

We are regularly launching new books in our series of practical day-to-day practitioners' guides. Visit our website and join our free newsletter to be kept informed and to receive special offers, free chapters, etc.

You can also follow us on Twitter at www.twitter.com/lawbriefpub.

Printed in Great Britain
by Amazon